Restructuring the SSI Disability Program for Children and Adolescents

Jerry L. Mashaw
James M. Perrin
and
Virginia P. Reno
Editors

Report of the Committee on Childhood
Disability of the Disability Policy Panel
Washington, D.C. 1996

NATIONAL
ACADEMY
OF·SOCIAL
INSURANCE

The National Academy of Social Insurance is a nonprofit, nonpartisan organization made up of the nation's leading experts on social insurance. Its mission is to conduct research and enhance public understanding of social insurance, to develop new leaders and to provide a nonpartisan forum for exchange of ideas on important issues in the field of social insurance. Social insurance, both in the United States and abroad, encompasses broad-based systems for insuring workers and their families against economic insecurity caused by loss of income from work and protecting individuals against the cost of personal health care services. The Academy's research covers social insurance systems, such as Social Security, unemployment insurance, workers' compensation and Medicare, and related social assistance and private employee benefits.

The Academy convenes study panels that are charged with conducting research, issuing findings and, in some cases, reaching recommendations based on their analyses. Panel members are selected for their recognized expertise and with due consideration for the balance of disciplines and perspectives appropriate to the project. The findings and any recommendations remain those of study panels and do not represent an official position of the Academy or its funders.

In accordance with procedures of the Academy, study panel reports are reviewed by a committee of the Board for completeness, accuracy, clarity and objectivity. The findings and recommendations in this report are those of the Committee on Childhood Disability of the Disability Policy Panel.

The project received financial support from The Pew Charitable Trusts, The Robert Wood Johnson Foundation and corporate members of the Health Insurance Association of America that offer long-term disability insurance.

© 1996 National Academy of Social Insurance

Library of Congress Catalog Card Number: 96-70003
ISBN 1-884902-06-5

The Disability Policy Panel

Jerry L. Mashaw, Chair,* Sterling Professor of Law
Institute of Social and Policy Studies
Yale University Law School, New Haven, CT

Monroe Berkowitz, Professor of Economics, Emeritus
Rutgers University, New Brunswick, NJ

Richard V. Burkhauser, Professor of Economics
Center for Policy Research, Maxwell School
Syracuse University, Syracuse, NY

Gerben DeJong, Director
National Rehabilitation Hospital-Research Center
Washington, DC

James N. Ellenberger, Assistant Director
Department of Occupational Safety and Health
AFL-CIO, Washington, DC

Lex Frieden, Senior Vice President
The Institute for Rehabilitation and Research
Houston, TX

Howard H. Goldman, M.D.,* Professor of Psychiatry
University of Maryland School of Medicine
Baltimore, MD

Arthur E. Hess, Consultant
Former Deputy Commissioner of Social Security
Charlottesville, VA

Thomas C. Joe, Director
Center for the Study of Social Policy, Washington, DC

Mitchell P. LaPlante, Associate Adjunct Professor
Institute for Health and Aging
University of California, San Francisco, CA

Douglas A. Martin, Special Assistant to the Chancellor
University of California, Los Angeles, CA

David Mechanic, Director
Institute for Health, Health Care Policy
  and Aging Research
Rutgers University, New Brunswick, NJ

Patricia M. Owens, President
Integrated Disability Management
UNUM America, Brooklyn, NY

James M. Perrin, M.D.,* Associate Professor of Pediatrics
Harvard Medical School
Massachusetts General Hospital, Boston, MA

Donald L. Shumway,* Co-director
RWJ Project on Developmental Disabilities
Institute on Disabilities
University of New Hampshire, Concord, NH

Susan S. Suter, President
World Institute on Disability, Oakland, CA

Eileen P. Sweeney,* Director of Government Affairs
Children's Defense Fund, Washington, DC

Jerry Thomas,* President
National Council of Disability Determination
Directors, Decatur, GA

---

* Committee on Childhood Disability

Disability Project Staff

Virginia P. Reno, Project Director

Kathryn Olson, Research Associate

Kathleen A. Brady, Project Associate

Suzanne Payne, Research Assistant

Elizabeth H. Esty, Consultant

Preface

The Disability Policy Project of the National Academy of Social Insurance began with a request from the Chairmen of the Committee on Ways and Means of the U.S. House of Representatives and its Social Security Subcommittee during the 102nd Congress. The Academy was asked to undertake a fundamental review of the Social Security disability programs, with particular emphasis on improving work outcomes for applicants, beneficiaries, and denied applicants for disability benefits. To do that, the Academy assembled a panel of leading experts on disability policy from varied disciplines and very different perspectives on disability policy.

This report was released in preliminary form in May 1995 and is being issued in final form along with the Panel's final report, *Balancing Security and Opportunity: The Challenge of Disability Income Policy.*

We accelerated our analysis of the children's Supplemental Security Income (SSI) program because legislative action affecting that program was on an urgent timetable in Congress. The Senate Finance Committee, congressional staff from that and other committees, administration officials, and the congressionally-mandated National Commission on Childhood Disability sought our advice on proposals before Congress.

We received assistance from many individuals and organizations in conducting this study. Experts from the Office of Disability of the Social Security Administration were particularly helpful in providing information and responding to our many questions about the program, its eligibility criteria and assessment techniques. We also consulted widely with clinical and research experts in the assessment of disability, including mental disorders, in children. We interviewed families about their experience seeking help for their children with disabilities and conducted focus groups with young adults and the parents of young adults who are recipients of SSI benefits.

This report originated in the Committee on Childhood Disability of the Panel, but it is supported by the overwhelming majority of the Panel. As might be expected for a topic of this complexity and a group representing diverse views, not every aspect of the draft is endorsed with unanimity. Some members of the Panel are attracted by the idea of further reducing the importance of cash benefits with respect to childhood disability in favor of an even more pronounced emphasis on services than is suggested in this report. On the other hand, there are those who believe that the continuation of cash benefits is not only essential, but that the Social Security Administration is already in the process of correcting the difficulties with the functional assessment of disability and that no further changes are needed in that regard. Those exceptions noted, the overwhelming majority of the Panel subscribes to the analysis and recommendations that follow.

Our overall position is relatively straightforward: We find that there is a strong rationale for the payment of cash benefits to families with disabled children. We view these payments in the context of needs for family support that include the special expenses of caring for a disabled child as well as the special limitations on family earnings that often attend the caretaking demands of a child with a severe disability. Particularly for some families with incomes sufficiently low to qualify for SSI, we believe that the margin provided by SSI cash payments is critical to the maintenance of the care of children in their own homes rather than in an institutional setting. And, we are strongly of the view that, both from a standpoint of the development of children and the potential cost to society, home care is the vastly preferred alternative.

The Panel is equally concerned that the payment of cash benefits be made only in appropriate cases; that those payments should not be excessive in the modest number of cases where families have more than one disabled child; and, most importantly, that the approach to the support of disabled children through the SSI program be reoriented toward an emphasis on the medical recovery, physical and mental development, and job readiness of children with disabilities. Wherever possible we believe that energetic measures should be taken by federal, state and local governments and private initiatives to limit the period within which cash support is necessary and to create transitions for children with disabilities to the world of work rather than to adult cash benefits programs.

In the pages that follow, we describe the nature and prevalence of childhood disability and our understanding of the underlying rationale for cash benefit payments in their current form. We then propose a series of reforms which include limiting benefits to families with more than one child with disabilities; strengthening the disability determination process to ensure that functional assessment is a technique that promotes accurate disability determinations; linking children receiving cash benefits with community-based services that will enhance their development; and strongly emphasizing the transition to work as children move from adolescence to adulthood.

The Panel has considered a broad range of other approaches to reform of the SSI program for children with disabilities. The possible use of vouchers or block grants to states for special services has received extensive consideration in our debates. In the end, the Committee and the vast majority of the Panel have found these alternatives either less efficacious in carrying out the purposes that we ascribe to the SSI program for children with disabilities or to have such severe implementation difficulties that they would be likely to fail their intended purposes.

Jerry L. Mashaw, Chair
Disability Policy Panel
Sterling Professor of Law
Yale University

Contents

OVERVIEW   1

Chapter 1   **THE COMMITTEE'S PERSPECTIVE**   7

Chapter 2   **THE NATURE AND PREVALENCE OF CHILDHOOD DISABILITY**   9
Prevalence of Childhood Disability   9
SSI Children Today: A Profile   9
Recent Growth Is Levelling Off   11
Families' Experience with Childhood Disability   13

Chapter 3   **RATIONALE FOR SSI BENEFITS FOR CHILDREN WITH DISABILITIES**   15
The Early Rationale is Stronger Today   15
Levelling the Playing Field: The Cost of Raising a Child with Disabilities   16
Family Support and Preservation   17
The Opportunity Costs of Care   17
Community Integration and Awareness   18
Choice of Methods of Support   18

Chapter 4   **BENEFITS FOR FAMILIES WITH MORE THAN ONE ELIGIBLE CHILD**   21

Chapter 5   **STRENGTHENING ELIGIBILITY CRITERIA**   23
Changing Composition of New Entrants to the Childhood Disability Rolls   23
Little Evidence of "Coaching" or Inaccurate Allowances   24
Recommendations to Strengthen the Functional Assessments   25
Caution Against Over-Reaction   29
Need for Longitudinal Evidence and Treatment Trials   30
Need for Better Diagnostic Data   31

Chapter 6 **YOUNG CHILDREN: LINKS WITH COMMUNITY-BASED SERVICES** 36
  The Landscape of Service Programs 33
  The Landscape from the Perspective of Families 36
  Recommendations 37

Chapter 7 **TRANSITION TO ADULTHOOD** 41
  The Young Adults' Perspective 41
  Transition Planning and Benefit Security for Teens 42

Appendix A 45
Appendix B 49
Panel Biographies 53
List of Abbreviations 57

Overview

The Committee on Childhood Disability of the Disability Policy Panel considered a broad range of alternatives to the Supplemental Security Income (SSI) benefit program for children with disabilities, including the possible use of vouchers or block grants to the states for services in lieu of cash support. In the end, we found these alternatives to be less efficacious in carrying out the purpose of SSI than the current structure or to have profound implementation pitfalls. The findings and recommendations set out below are based on the view that it is neither necessary nor practical to fundamentally restructure SSI for disabled children. At the same time, we propose a number of changes to strengthen eligibility criteria, limit family benefit amounts and reorient the program toward the medical recovery, physical and mental development, and job readiness of children with disabilities.

The Childhood Disability Program

In December, 1994, some 837,000 children under age 18 were receiving SSI benefits. These children share two common realities: they have significant disabilities and very low incomes. Mental retardation is the primary diagnosis for about half the school-age children who receive SSI. Others have significant physical or other mental disorders.

The number of children awarded SSI benefits grew rapidly between 1989 and 1993, but has since declined. The growth in 1989-93 is attributed to four factors: the 1990 Supreme Court decision in *Sullivan* v. *Zebley,* which changed the assessment of childhood disability and required that past claims which had been denied be reassessed; the update of the listings of disabling childhood mental impairments in 1990; legislatively mandated outreach activities by the Social Security Administration (SSA) as well as efforts by states and private organizations to enroll eligible children in SSI; and an economic recession in 1990-91 that caused more families with disabled children to meet the program's low-income criteria.

The rapid growth in the program has slowed. Fewer children were awarded SSI disability in 1994 than in 1993.

Rationale for SSI for Children with Disabilities

When SSI was enacted in 1972, its main purpose was to assure a basic minimum income for needy aged, blind and disabled individuals who, under the prior programs of federal grants to states, were subject to very disparate treatment across the nation because of great disparities among states in their financial capacity or willingness to provide such support. The prior law had provided federal funds to states for children who were blind, but not for other disabled children. The question arose whether the new federal SSI program should include blind and disabled children.

Then and now, the rationale for including children in SSI is somewhat different from that for adults. Cash assistance for poor adults who are aged or disabled is justified because they lack the capacity to support themselves through their own earnings. That is true for all poor children. For low-income children with disabilities, however, there are added justifications for support. Their disabilities pose additional costs to their families and, if they do not have appropriate developmental supports when they are young, they are at high risk of relying on public support when they become adults.

In brief, there is a clear rationale and a compelling need for cash support to families with a disabled child. The basic purpose of these benefits is to support and preserve the capacity of families to care for their disabled children in their own homes by:

- Meeting some of the additional disability-related costs of raising a disabled child (examples are listed in chapter 3 of the report);
- Compensating for some of the income lost because of the everyday necessities of caring for a disabled child; and
- Meeting the child's basic needs for food, clothing and shelter.

Without these supports, disabled children would be at a much greater risk of losing both a secure home environment and the best opportunity for integration into community life, including the world of work.

Families with More than One Child with Disabilities

Families with more than one child who qualifies for SSI are rare. In such cases, a full SSI benefit is payable to each eligible child. We believe SSI payments to such families should be calibrated to recognize economies of scale in shared living arrangements.

SSI benefits for families with more than one disabled child should be limited to 1.5 times the individual benefit for two children and 2.0 times the individual benefit for three or more children, with appropriate exceptions to those limits for "Katie Beckett" children (who require round-the-clock nursing care), foster care families and adopted special-needs children. No disabled child should lose Medicaid eligibility because of this limit on cash benefits for the family.

Allegations About Coaching

We examined concerns about motivational issues related to payment of benefits based on mental disorders, including allegations that parents coach their children to misbehave or perform poorly in school so that they can qualify for benefits. Any evidence of such coaching or "gaming the system" is extraordinarily thin — and appears to be based on anecdotes or perceptions of dubious benefit claims, which upon investigation are found to have been denied. Furthermore, SSA in 1994 took rigorous new steps to investigate and rectify, when necessary, all allegations of inappropriate benefit claims. The number of such cases reported to date is very small.

Strengthening Disability Eligibility Criteria

Assessing the limitations in functioning caused by a medical impairment strengthens and improves the determination of disability for SSI eligibility. Nevertheless, functional assessment techniques are far from perfect. They often use less than the best evidence, and there is a potential for "double counting," whereby a particular limitation may be counted twice in evaluating functional capacity. These issues can and should be remedied through changes in SSA regulations.

Our recommendation would require SSA to revise a portion of its regulations for assessing childhood disability and to apply the new criteria to all future claims. The changes, themselves, would not require Congress to amend the Social Security Act. Congress could, however, require and set a timetable for the regulatory change as a way to clarify its intent and SSA's authority to strengthen, and in some ways tighten, the eligibility criteria for future SSI applicants.

The recommendation would modify both SSA's medical listings for childhood mental disorders and the individualized functional assessment (IFA). The medical listings are 100 or so specific mental or physical impairments described in regulations. If a claimant's impairment matches a listed condition or is medically equivalent to a listed condition, benefits are allowed. If a child's impairment(s) does not meet the listing, an IFA is done to determine if the functional limitations resulting from the child's condition cause him or her to be disabled. The IFA was implemented to comply with the Supreme Court's 1990 decision in *Sullivan* v. *Zebley*. The specific modifications follow:

1. Eliminate maladaptive behavior as a separate domain in the functional assessment in the childhood mental disorders listings and the IFA.

Maladaptive behavior is a genuine attribute of severe mental retardation or mental illness for some individuals. We believe that children with severe mental disorders can and should still qualify based on other diagnostic and functional criteria. Eliminating maladaptive behavior as a separate domain in the functional assessment would eliminate the possibility of double counting deficits in behavioral and other functional domains. It would also avoid any mistaken perception that inappropriate behavior, in and of itself, is a basis for receiving SSI benefits.

2. Increase the use of standardized tests to assess the functional consequences of mental disorders.

Greater use of standardized tests can improve the quality of evidence used to assess the disabling consequences of childhood mental disorders.

3. Revamp the IFA to assess children's overall disability using criteria that are not so similar to those used in the mental disorders listings and that are appropriate for children with physical impairments as well as for children who have both mental and physical impairments.

The current IFA is problematic because it is too similar to the functional assessment used to evaluate mental disorders. Consequently, it is used mainly to allow benefits based on mental disorders. The IFA should be replaced with a global assessment that is qualitatively different from that used for mental disorders and that is appropriate for children with physical impairments or illnesses as well as mental conditions.

New regulations should be developed expeditiously to strengthen the childhood eligibility criteria. At the same time, care should be taken not to repeat the tumult of the early 1980s, when radical retrenchment in federal disability policy brought widespread individual hardship and judicial challenges. States were at first reluctant, and then refused, to implement the harsh policies because it left them with the burden of care for vulnerable populations whose federal disability benefits were denied or terminated.

Need for Longitudinal Evidence and Treatment Trials

When a child's condition appears to meet the disability criteria and longitudinal medical records are needed to confirm the diagnosis, but such records are lacking, a provisional benefit would be appropriate. During a period of, say, 12 months, SSI benefits and Medicaid would be provided on a provisional basis, with a review scheduled at the end of the period. The review would be based on whether the child's condition meets the statutory definition of disability. SSA would not be required to demonstrate that medical improvement had occurred, as is now required in most reviews of continuing disability.

Provisional benefits are also appropriate when medical evidence suggests that treatment could alleviate the disabling consequences of the child's condition. After the limited period, the review of the child's condition would be based on evidence that treatment had been tried and on the remaining functional consequences of the disorder.

If the disabling consequences of the child's condition are remedied by appropriate treatment, SSI benefits should end. If the diagnosis remains, but its disabling consequences were controlled by treatment, Medicaid should remain available to ensure continued access to the needed medical treatment.

Need for Better Diagnostic Data

Because there is significant co-morbidity in childhood disorders, particularly mental disorders, existing data on the primary diagnosis of children allowed benefits often fails to convey the full nature of the child's impairments. In addition, there are concerns about the accuracy of SSA's procedures for recording diagnostic codes for primary, secondary and tertiary conditions among children.

Measures should be taken to ensure the accuracy of childhood disability primary and secondary diagnostic codes as well as outcomes of functional evaluations. These codes and indicators should be included in data files available for evaluating trends in the SSI program and its beneficiaries.

Young Children: Links with Community-Based Services

A variety of community-based programs funded by a mix of federal, state, local and private monies offer various services to children with disabilities. The major public programs include Medicaid, the Maternal and Child Health program, special education, Part H Early Intervention, and planning and advocacy for children and adults with developmental disabilities.

These community-based services and programs are often fragmented, uneven in their availability, and extremely difficult to navigate, according to parents from all walks of life and all income levels who have sought the services their disabled children need. For low-income parents, the need for assistance in navigating these service networks is particularly acute.

SSI cash assistance for infants and young children should be coordinated with existing community-based programs designed to enhance the child's prospects for healthy development.

- If SSA is not equipped to obtain information about local programs or answer questions about them, that information and referral role should be filled under contract with private or other public agencies.
- Private or local public organizations, under contract with SSA or some other agency, could assemble user-friendly information packets about various local or national service networks available to families of children with different types of disabilities.
- SSA would be responsible for having the informational materials available in its local district offices, but questions about it would be referred to the contractor who assembled the information.

Furthermore, states and localities should be encouraged to develop a working consortium among the agencies serving children with disabilities, with clear allocation of responsibility for service coordination for specific categories of children receiving SSI. They should coordinate with parent groups, the state agency that evaluates disability for SSA and SSA field offices, as appropriate.

Children's progress should be tracked and periodically reviewed by SSA to ensure that those who recover do not remain on the SSI disability rolls and that those whose disabilities persist are linked to services appropriate to their changing needs as they grow older.

Transition to Adulthood

Programs in high school should prepare teenagers with disabilities for productive employment to the maximum extent possible. Under the Individuals with Disabilities Education Act, the federal government required in 1990, for the first time, that all students in special education programs receive transition services by the age of 16. The following recommendations build on the special education requirements for transition planning.

At age 14, teenagers on SSI, together with their parents and special education advisors, should develop transition plans and, where appropriate, set career goals. The plan would set a track for the child's educational goals for the remainder of secondary school and should include: (1) academic preparation for attending college; or (2) vocational preparation that includes survey courses as well as concentration in the target vocational goal; and (3) preparation for life skills and independent living as adults.

Transition planning between ages 14 and 18 should also provide information about SSI work incentives which can be used to pursue vocational goals. While they are pursuing their goals for work or further education after high school, young people should have assurance of SSI benefit security until they reach age 18, even if they begin to demonstrate work skills.

Finally, transition planning should explain the current requirement that young people receiving SSI will have a continuing disability review, subject to the adult disability criteria, when they reach age 18. It should be explained to the child and parents that, if the child's impairment(s) does not meet the adult criteria, benefits will be discontinued.

Chapter 1 The Committee's Perspective

While the Disability Policy Panel's main focus is on the disability benefit programs for adults, the Panel and its Committee on Childhood Disability have examined the Supplemental Security Income (SSI) provisions for children with disabilities in low-income families. After consulting with federal policy officials and congressional staff early in the project, we concluded that our first task in reviewing the SSI childhood disability program should be to examine the rationale for such a program. For this task we reviewed the very limited existing research on the SSI childhood disability program and commissioned new field research to learn the experience of families and of state, local and private service providers and others involved in aiding families of children with significant disabilities. We also conducted focus groups with young adults receiving SSI and their parents, and consulted widely with experts in childhood disability, including experts in childhood mental disorders.

Our recommendations are based on several broad findings about the nature of childhood disability. First, despite a common lay view that many children with disabilities face early death, the reality is that the vast majority of children with cognitive, physical or mental disabilities survive to young adulthood.[1] Furthermore, many such children and adolescents can be educated, maintain important personal relationships and become productively employed as adults. Thus, a central goal of disability policy must be to encourage the growth and development of children with disabilities and their integration to the extent possible in all aspects of American life as young adults. Substantial numbers of young people with disabilities should not require ongoing SSI benefits when they become young adults.[2] The current SSI program provides needed cash support, and for most children, essential medical assistance. Nonetheless, the long term growth and development of childhood beneficiaries and their independence from public support can be more effectively achieved by linking payment of SSI benefits with appropriate treatment and services.

---

1. S. Gortmaker and W. Sappenfield, "Chronic Childhood Disorders: Prevalence and Impact," *Pediatric Clinics of North America*, vol. 31, 1984, pp. 3-18; and P.W. Newacheck and W.R. Taylor, "Childhood Chronic Illness: Prevalence, Severity, and Impact," *American Journal of Public Health*, vol. 82, 1992, pp. 364-71.
2. M. Hack, et al., "School-age Outcomes in Children with Birth Weights Under 750 Grams," *New England Journal of Medicine*, vol. 331, 1994, pp. 753-59; M. Hack, et al., "Health of Very Low Birth Weight Children During their First Eight Years," *Journal of Pediatrics*, vol. 122, 1993, pp. 887-92; M. Hack, et al., "The Effect of Very Low Birth Weight and Social Risk of Neuro-cognitive Abilities at School Age," *Journal of Developmental and Behavioral Pediatrics*, vol. 13, 1992, pp. 412-20; B.R. Vohr, et al., "Neurodevelopmental and Medical Status of Low Birthweight Survivors of Bronchopulmonary Dysplasia at 10 to 12 Years of Age," *Developmental Medicine and Child Neurology*, vol. 33, 1991, pp. 690-97; S.L. Gortmaker, et al., "An Unexpected Success Story: Transition to Adulthood of Youth with Chronic Physical Health Conditions," *Journal of Research on Adolescence*, vol. 3, 1993, pp. 317-36; I.B. Pless, et al., "Long-term Sequelae of Chronic Physical Disorders in Childhood," *Pediatrics*, vol. 91, 1993, pp. 1131-36; and I.B. Pless and M.E.J. Wadsworth, "Long-term Effects of Chronic Illness on Young Adults," in R.E.K. Stein (ed.), *Caring for Children With Chronic Illness* (New York: Springer Publishing, 1989), pp. 147-158.

Second, early intervention with appropriate family supports and services is effective. Increasing evidence shows that providing family support and services early to children diminishes long-term disability and dependence on public institutions.[3] Appropriate assistance to families and children can also prevent secondary disabilities — that is, prevention of additional disabilities secondary to the primary clinical problem. For example, the family whose child was born at 1000 grams (less than 3 pounds) and had some intracranial bleeding and pulmonary disease will likely be eligible for both SSI and early intervention. Yet, with family support and appropriate services, this child will likely have limited disability and need substantially less support as she grows.

Third, family support and preservation should be a fundamental goal of public policy. For many families, caring for a child with disabilities requires substantial expenditures of time and money, limiting out-of-home employment for family members. SSI support can prevent the breakup of families resulting from institutional placement of their child (or foster care) and enhances families' abilities to nurture their own children. Further, the burden of caring for a child with disabilities places strains on all family members and too often results in marital dissolution. SSI support, which is available to two-parent families as well as one-parent families, alleviates some of the financial stress associated with caring for a disabled child.

Finally, we are mindful of concerns about motivational issues surrounding the payment of cash benefits to families whose children perform poorly due to certain types of mental or behavioral disorders. We are recommending changes in the Social Security Administration's (SSA) disability criteria and family benefit levels to address these concerns. We also recognize there are concerns that policies providing income support to low-income families of children with disabilities may pose an incentive for poor families to have their children classified as disabled.[4]

We believe that these concerns can and should be addressed by recommended changes in eligibility criteria, family benefit amounts and provisions linking SSI children with appropriate treatment and services.

The next chapter of this report provides background on childhood disability and the SSI program. It reviews estimates of the prevalence of childhood disability, gives a profile of low-income children receiving SSI benefits, and outlines the reasons for the growth in the SSI childhood rolls which began in 1990 and has now levelled off or declined. It also reports findings from field research and focus groups about the experience of families caring for their children with disabilities. The rest of this report states our findings and recommendations.

---

3. J.P. Shonkoff, et al., "Development of Infants with Disabilities and their Families: Implications for Theory and Service Delivery," *Monograph of the Society for Research in Child Development*, vol. 57, 1992, pp. 1-153; J.P. Shonkoff and P. Hauser-Cram, "Early Intervention for Disabled Infants and their Families: A Quantitative Analysis," *Pediatrics*, vol. 80, 1987, pp. 650-58; and Infant Health and Development Program, "Enhancing the Outcomes of Low Birth Weight, Premature Infants: A Multi-site Randomized Trial," *Journal of the American Medical Association*, vol. 263, 1990, pp. 3035-42.
4. C. Weaver, "Welfare Payments to the Disabled, Making America Sick," *The American Enterprise*, December 1994.

Chapter 2: The Nature and Prevalence of Childhood Disability

Prevalence of Childhood Disability

The population of children with disabilities is small, but significant, and varies depending on the definition of disability used. The National Health Interview Survey estimates that in 1993, children who had a "limitation in their major activity" — which means attending school for children ages 5-17, or playing for younger children — numbered 3.1 million, or 4.6 percent of children under 18.[5] The U.S. Department of Education estimates that in school year 1992-93, the number of children ages 6-21 enrolled in some form of special education was about 4.6 million. The special education definition is more expansive: just over half had learning disabilities and nearly a quarter had speech or language impairments. Mental retardation, serious emotional disturbance and all other disabilities including blindness, hearing impairments and physical disabilities, together, accounted for 27 percent of the special education population.[6]

In December of 1994, there were 837,000 low-income children under 18 receiving SSI. The number of children receiving SSI is much smaller than either the number of children enrolled in special education or the number of children with limitations in their major activity for two reasons.

First, SSI has a strict test of disability. To qualify for SSI benefits, the statute requires that children must have a medically determinable physical or mental impairment of comparable severity to that which would make an adult unable to engage in any substantial gainful activity. The test of comparable severity that was put in regulations to comply with the Supreme Court's 1990 decision in *Sullivan* v. *Zebley*[7] requires that children be substantially limited in their ability to function independently, appropriately and effectively in an age-appropriate manner.

Second, SSI is paid only to children in low-income families. The income and resource limits take into account the income of parents and the presence of other children in the household. SSI benefits are reduced as family income rises. Income thresholds are lower for smaller families or for families whose income is from sources other than earnings, such as Social Security benefits or veteran's compensation.

SSI Children Today: A Profile

While there is great diversity within the SSI childhood population, they share two common realities: they live in low-income households and they have medically determined impairments that limit their ability to function.

---

5. National Health Interview Survey, 1993.
6. U.S. Department of Education, *Sixteenth Annual Report to Congress on the Implementation of the Individuals with Disabilities Education Act* (Washington DC: U.S. Government Printing Office, 1994), table 1.4, p. 9.
7. *Sullivan* v. *Zebley*, 493 U.S. 521 (1990).

Table 2-1. Children Receiving SSI, by Primary Diagnosis and Age, December 1994

Diagnostic group	Total	Under 3 years	3-5 years	6-12 years	13-17 years
Total number	836,910	62,090	120,990	348,410	269,420
Total with diagnosis	701,360	50,160	103,390	328,010	219,800
Total percent	100.0	100.0	100.0	100.0	100.0
Mental retardation	42.6	7.2	26.8	45.6	53.7
Other mental and emotional disorders	23.4	7.1	17.6	25.3	27.0
Physical disorders—subtotal	34.0	85.8	55.5	29.2	19.2
Nervous system and sense organs	12.3	14.5	19.0	12.3	8.5
Respiratory system	2.8	6.4	5.5	2.3	1.3
Infectious and parasitic diseases	0.4	1.1	0.8	0.3	0.1
Neoplasms	1.6	1.5	2.4	1.7	1.2
Endocrine, nutritional, and metabolic	1.0	1.5	1.4	0.9	1.0
Circulatory system	0.7	2.8	1.4	0.4	0.4
Digestive system	0.3	1.1	0.8	0.2	0.1
Musculoskeletal system and connective tissue	1.2	1.2	1.3	1.1	1.2
Congenital anomalies	4.6	18.8	8.6	3.3	1.6
Other	9.1	36.9	14.3	6.7	3.8

Abbreviation: SSI = Supplemental Security Income.
Source: Social Security Administration, *Children Receiving SSI*, December 1994, table 4, p. 10.

Types of Disabilities. Among children receiving SSI, the most common primary diagnosis was mental retardation, accounting for 43 percent of all such children in December, 1994 (table 2-1). The second most common diagnosis was a mental disorder other than mental retardation, which accounted for 23 percent of SSI children. These mental impairments include: organic mental disorders, schizophrenia, depression, manic and bipolar disorders, autism, attention deficit hyperactivity disorder (ADHD), learning and communication disorders, and behavioral disorders. Impairments of the nervous system (such as cerebral palsy, epilepsy and other nervous system disorders) and sensory impairments (such as vision and hearing disorders) were the primary diagnosis for 12 percent of SSI children. Respiratory disorders account for 3 percent. Diseases of the circulatory, digestive or musculoskeletal system, infectious diseases, neoplasms, and endocrine and metabolic disorders, combined, were the primary diagnoses for 5 percent. Congenital anomalies and other disorders were the primary diagnostic codes for 14 percent of SSI children.

The difference in disabling conditions among age groups reflects the dynamic nature of childhood disability. Often it is difficult to have a precise diagnosis for newborns or very young children. Among infants and toddlers under the age of 3, over half (56 percent) have as their primary diagnosis congenital anomalies (Down syndrome, congenital heart anomalies, or multiple dysfunctions) or other disorders (such as very low birth-weight, growth impairments). Among children of elementary school age, nearly half (46 percent) had mental retardation as their primary diagnosis, while among teenagers, 54 percent had mental retardation as their primary diagnosis.

Living Arrangements. The large majority of children who receive SSI live with one or both parents — although a minority reside in institutions or in foster care. In December 1994, 80 percent of SSI children lived with their parents, including 30 percent who lived with both parents. Those not living with parents include a small number (about 1 percent) who live in Medicaid institutions. The rest live with other relatives, in foster care, or on their own.[8]

Benefit Levels. The maximum federal SSI benefit for a disabled child is $458 per month in 1995. That benefit is reduced dollar for dollar for the family's other countable income that is attributable to the child. The large majority (68 percent) of disabled children receiving SSI receive the full federal benefit, which indicates that they and their families have very limited income.[9]

---

8. Social Security Administration, *Children Receiving SSI*, December 1994, p. 2 and p. 15.
9. In 1995, for a family of four — a disabled child, a sibling and two parents, where all income is from the parents' earnings — full benefits are paid if earnings are less than $1,728 per month (about $20,700 annually); they are reduced to zero once earnings reach $2,644 ($31,700 annually). Income thresholds are lower if countable family income is from sources other than earnings, such as Social Security or veteran's compensation. For example, for a family of three — a disabled child, a sibling and one parent — full benefits are paid if family income is less than $727 per month ($8,700 annually); they are reduced to zero once countable unearned income reaches $1,185 ($14,200 annually). Social Security Administration, Office of Program Benefits Policy.
10. These include: whereabouts unknown, presumptive payments end, lack of representative payee, entering a public (non-Medicaid) institution, failure to furnish report, outside the U.S., record composition change, and other. Social Security Administration, Office of Supplemental Security Income.

Table 2-2. Number of Children Receiving SSI, 1988-1994

Year[a]	Total receiving SSI[b]	New benefit awards in the year[b]
1988	290,256	51,193
1989	296,298	54,497
1990	340,230	82,753
1991	438,853	125,821
1992	623,845	191,054
1993	770,501	225,611
1994	892,543	205,626

a. Total number of beneficiaries are for December of each year.
b. Totals include some recipients ages 18-21 who receive benefits as children.
Abbreviation: SSI = Supplemental Security Income.
Sources: Social Security Administration, *Children Receiving SSI*, December 1994, table 1, p. 6; and Social Security Administration, *Annual Statistical Supplement to the Social Security Bulletin* (Washington, DC: U.S. Government Printing Office, 1994), table 7.A8, p. 288.

Recent Growth Is Levelling Off

The number of children entering the SSI childhood disability rolls grew rapidly after 1989 as a result of policy changes emanating from legislative and judicial requirements combined with a recession and state initiatives. The growth in childhood disability awards, however, has levelled off and actually declined in 1994. Fewer children entered the SSI rolls in 1994 than in 1993 (table 2-2).

Not all children who receive SSI remain on the rolls indefinitely. Children who left the rolls for at least one month numbered 100,900 in 1993 and 84,300 in 1992, while children who left and remained off the rolls for at least 12 months numbered 29,300 in 1992. The most common reason they left and remained off the rolls was an increase in family income, which accounted for 55 percent of those off the rolls for at least a year. Other reasons were the death of the child (15 percent), excess family resources (6 percent), entering a Medicaid institution (2 percent), recovery (1 percent), and various other reasons.[10]

The growth in the number of children receiving SSI benefits can be traced to three distinct policy changes: the update of the medical listings[11] of the childhood mental disorders in December 1990 that followed legislatively-mandated updates in the listings of adult mental disorders; implementation of the Supreme Court decision *Sullivan* v. *Zebley* in February 1990; and legislatively-mandated outreach activities by SSA as well as private efforts to enroll eligible children in the SSI program. In addition, an economic recession and state initiatives contributed to the growth.

Update of Mental Disorders Listings in 1990. The update of the childhood mental disorders listings in December 1990 was based on the same conceptual framework used to update the adult mental disorders listings in 1985. The change for adults was required by court decisions in the early 1980s and by legislation enacted in 1984 that required the new mental impairment criteria to focus on evaluating the person's ability to perform substantial gainful activity in a competitive workplace environment. The new childhood listings emphasized functional criteria (like the adult mental listings published in 1985), and added new listings for certain specific conditions, such as ADHD, for children.

1990 Supreme Court Decision in *Sullivan* v. *Zebley*. The U.S. Supreme Court decision in *Sullivan* v. *Zebley* in February 1990 expanded SSI eligibility criteria for children. *Zebley* created a temporary bulge in awards as SSA readjudicated denied claims back to 1980. To date, some 91,500 new awards have been made as a result of these readjudications.[12] The expanded eligibility criteria also caused an increase in the level of new applications and awards.

---

11. The "medical listings" are 100 or so specific mental or physical conditions described in regulations. If the claimant's impairment matches the listed condition or is medically equivalent to a listed condition, benefits are allowed.
12. Social Security Administration, Office of Programs, Policy, Evaluation and Communications.
13. Section 1614(a)(3)(A) of the Social Security Act.
14. Section 8008 of the Omnibus Budget Reconciliation Act of 1989.

When the SSI program was enacted in 1972, the law provided that children would be considered disabled for SSI purposes if they suffered from "any medically determinable physical or mental impairment of comparable severity" to that which would make an adult disabled.[13] Before the *Zebley* decision, childhood disability had been determined using only medical listings. A special set of medical listings had been developed for children, and children were found disabled if their condition met or equalled conditions found in either the medical listings for adults or the special childhood disability listings.

For adults whose impairments do not meet the medical listings, there is an additional step. The adult's "residual functional capacity" is evaluated and used to determine whether the claimant is able to do his or her past work, or any other work which exists in significant numbers in the national economy. There was no counterpart to the "residual functional capacity" assessment for children. In *Zebley*, the Supreme Court found that this did not meet the statutory requirement for determining "comparable severity." The regulations implementing the *Zebley* decision were issued in February 1991 and specified that children whose impairments did not meet or equal the medical listings would undergo an individualized functional assessment (IFA), as called for in the Supreme Court decision, to determine whether their impairments substantially limit their ability to function independently, appropriately, and effectively in an age-appropriate manner.

Outreach Required by Law. Widespread publicity followed the Court's decision, and concerted efforts were made by SSA and by private groups to enroll eligible children in the SSI program. Legislation enacted by Congress in 1989 stipulated that SSA should have an ongoing outreach initiative to enroll children in the SSI program.[14]

Economic Recession and State Initiatives. After seven years of sustained economic growth, the recession of 1990-1991 coincided with the policy changes described above. As parents lost their jobs and depleted their savings, more children with disabilities met the low-income and resource eligibility criteria of the SSI program.

In addition to SSA's outreach efforts, state and local governments have developed initiatives to screen for SSI eligible children in foster care, those on Aid to Families with Dependent Children and other special needs children. These activities increase claims for SSI benefits. To the extent that the children meet SSI criteria and receive benefits, the benefits improve their incomes and, in some cases, reduce expenditures of state or local governments.

Families' Experience with Childhood Disability

We learned from interviews with families and service providers of the special demands that children's disabilities place on their families. The stresses include physical and emotional burdens, out-of-pocket costs and foregone earnings. Field research commissioned for the project reports:[15]

- While parents struggle to find sources of assistance, they must cope with the daily demands of physical care on their own. That care may include having to suction your baby girl's throat every 15 minutes to keep it clear for breathing; or carrying your son in his full-body neck to hip cast; or changing your eight-year-old son's diapers because he is not yet toilet trained. On top of these sorts of day-in and day-out demands come frequent trips to doctors, therapists, and hospitals.

- The burden of daily care falls on both parents, but among those interviewed in this study, the burden bore most heavily on mothers. The mothers often had left their jobs to become full-time caretakers for their disabled children. Leaving a job means not only disrupting one's career, but losing an income. One of the major strains of caring for a child with a disability is financial. Out-of-pocket expenses for health care, related services, special clothing or equipment, or respite care can be considerable.

- All the pressures of raising a child with a disability put an enormous emotional strain on parents as individuals and on the bonds that hold marriages together. Some of the parents interviewed for this study report that they became divorced or separated from their spouses as a result of the tension of caring for a disabled child. More systematic studies indicate this is not uncommon.[16]

The project also conducted focus groups with beneficiaries, including young adults receiving SSI and family members of such young adult beneficiaries. Screening for participation in the focus groups required that participants be able to speak for themselves and get to the focus group site.[17] Some of the young adult beneficiaries had profound health problems or disabilities that ruled out their ability to participate in a focus group and, in many cases, in competitive employment. The interviews with parents of young adult beneficiaries provide a family perspective on how they had dealt with the burden of daily care when their children were young, and how it continued as their children grew older.

My daughter had brain cancer when she was two. She just turned 20. She is three feet tall and weighs 50 pounds and needs 24-hour care.... If I had $10 for every time we were told she would not make it through the night, I would be rich.... When a person needs 24-hour care, thank God there are two parents in the household. I would go crazy if I didn't work some. I work six months, then my wife works six months. (father, Portland, OR)

My son, age 19, had a brain tumor and stroke when he was 11. A good life for him is built around people he knows care. He can sense whether a person likes him or

---

15. J.G. Cedarbaum, "Policies for Children with Disabilities: Connecticut, Virginia and Some National Trends," working paper prepared for the Disability Policy Panel, January 1995, p. 32.
16. Ibid., p. 33; and J. Mauldon, "Children's Risks of Experiencing Divorce and Remarriage: Do Disabled Children Destabilize Marriages?" *Population Studies*, vol. 46, 1992, pp. 349-62.
17. Interviews with the young adults, themselves, are in chapter 6.

not. Or will be mean or not. He responds meanly if a person is mean to him. I could put him in a foster home. I won't do that. SSI is not enough. He is a sweet, loving teddy bear. He is nonverbal. 24-hour a day care is essential. Many people don't understand that. (mother, Portland, OR)

My daughter was born with a visual impairment. She had a stroke when she was three. She will be 19.... She understands simple commands, simple terms. She gets frustrated. She is nonverbal. We taught her appropriate-type touching. She responds to hugging. We direct her by shoulder rubs. (mother, Des Moines, IA)

Chapter 3 Rationale for SSI Benefits for Children with Disabilities

When SSI was enacted in 1972, its main purpose was to assure a basic minimum income for needy, aged, blind and disabled individuals who, under the prior programs of federal grants to states,[18] were subject to very different treatment across the nation because of great disparities among states in their financial capacity or willingness to provide such support. The prior law had allowed federal matching funds to states for children who were blind, but not for other disabled children. The question arose whether the new federal SSI program should include blind and disabled children.

The Early Rationale is Stronger Today

Then and now, the rationale for including children in SSI is somewhat different from that for adults. Cash assistance for poor adults who are aged or disabled is justified because they lack the capacity to support themselves through their own earnings. That is true for all poor children. For low-income children with disabilities, however, there are added justifications for support. Their disabilities pose additional costs to their families and, if they do not have appropriate developmental supports when they are young, they are at high risk of relying on public support when they become adults.

The House Ways and Means Committee in 1971 argued for including children with disabilities in the new SSI program on grounds that: "disabled children living in low-income households are among the most disadvantaged of all Americans and are deserving of special assistance in order to help them become self-supporting members of our society. ...[P]oor children with disabilities should be eligible for SSI benefits because their needs are often greater than those of nondisabled children."[19] The Senate Finance Committee at the time opposed including children in the SSI program on grounds that disabled children's needs were greater only in the area of health care, which could be provided by Medicaid.[20]

SSI does not duplicate other programs which may serve some low-income children, such as Aid to Families with Dependent Children (AFDC) or Medicaid, because the needs of disabled children and their families go beyond what is provided by these programs. For example, AFDC is provided mostly to single-parent families where no adults are em-

---

18. The prior programs were Old Age Assistance and Aid to the Blind, enacted in 1935, and Aid to the Permanently and Totally Disabled, enacted in 1950. The federal law set broad guidelines and authorized federal matching funds to the states, which set eligibility criteria and benefit amounts and administered the programs.
19. U.S. House of Representatives, *Social Security Amendments of 1971, Report of the Ways and Means Committee on H.R. 1*, H. Rpt. No. 92-231 (Washington, DC: U.S. Government Printing Office, May 26, 1971), pp. 146-148.
20. U.S. Senate, *Social Security Amendments of 1972, Report of the Committee on Finance, U.S. Senate to Accompany H.R. 1*, S. Rpt. No. 92-1230 (Washington, DC: U.S. Government Printing Office, September 26, 1972), pp. 384-86.

ployed. Its benefit is intended to support an entire family, and it does not recognize the added costs of a child with a disability.[21] Medicaid programs vary tremendously from state to state in terms of the services covered and who is eligible. They do not meet all of the disability-related needs of a disabled child.

Since SSI was enacted, three important changes in the nature and environment of childhood disability strengthen the rationale originally offered by the Ways and Means Committee.

- First, because of medical advances, more children with major disabilities are surviving to young adulthood. With appropriate nurturing and support, increasing numbers have the ability to enter the work force when they become adults.

- Second, there is far greater expectation now, than 20 or 30 years ago, that children with significant disabilities should be cared for in their own homes by their own families, rather than in institutions or out-of-home placements. Being raised in a caring home environment is far better for the child, and is a significant savings to the public fisc, but it is a financial and emotional burden on families who draw the lot of caring for a child with disabilities.

- Third, there is an increasing expectation, if not financial necessity, that both mothers and fathers will be in the paid work force. To care for a disabled child at home often necessitates either the opportunity cost of foregoing all or part of one parent's earnings, or paying for a level of trained child care that is beyond the means of most families, and certainly those of modest income.

---

21. Under AFDC rules, a disabled child who receives SSI is not counted in the AFDC unit and does not qualify for AFDC. He or she is disregarded when determining the AFDC benefit level. U.S. House of Representatives, Committee on Ways and Means, *Overview of Entitlement Programs (1994 Green Book)*, WMCP: 103-27 (Washington, DC: U.S. Government Printing Office, July 1994), p. 334 and p. 337.

We find there is a clear rationale and compelling need for a federal program of cash support for low-income families of children with severe disabilities. That rationale, which is elaborated below, is to level the playing field between families with disabled children and others by meeting some of the added disability-related costs of care as well as basic necessities; to promote family preservation; to compensate for some of the opportunity costs of foregone earnings to care for a disabled child; and to promote community integration and awareness, with long-term beneficial results for both the child and the community.

Levelling the Playing Field: The Cost of Raising a Child with Disabilities

As suggested in snapshots from field research and focus groups, there are myriad special burdens placed on families of children with severe disabilities. Cash support can ease those burdens, even if it cannot remove them.

The added financial burden includes many items that are not covered by traditional health care coverage, Medicaid or other public programs. The following list illustrates some of the diverse needs of disabled children:

- highly-trained child care providers for children with severe mental illness who require extensive supervision;

- substitute providers of paramedical care that parents learn to give but cannot always provide 24 hours-a-day;

- specially-adapted shoes or clothing for children whose bodies don't match standard clothing;

- diapers and clothing to accommodate older children who are not yet toilet trained;

- specialized toys and educational equipment for children who cannot manipulate typical equipment;

- tools to facilitate communication, such as flashcards, pictures, and computers;

- modifications to the home and specialized furniture and equipment to accommodate the child's impairment and facilitate independence;

- alternative foods for restricted diets;

- transportation to school, doctor and therapy appointments for children who cannot ride in the seats of a standard car, or whose family do not have cars, or who cannot use public transportation;

- training for parents to cope with the demands of bringing up a severely mentally ill child, avoid out-of-home placement and help the child to reach his or her fullest potential;

- replacement of furniture, appliances, walls and doors damaged or worn out as a result of a child's impairment; and

- respite care for the child so that parents can attend to their own needs and those of other members of the family.

Even the best health insurance plan or Medicaid does not cover all of the medical costs incurred by disabled children. For example, there may be strict limits on psychiatric treatment, medical supplies and some durable medical equipment might be excluded, or benefit caps may be reached.

Moreover, SSI children are in low-income families. Low-income families have even fewer resources to cope with the special needs of their children. The SSI benefit often must be used to meet basic needs such as food, clothing and shelter in order to provide a stable home environment for the child. For a child with physical or mental disabilities, growing up poor is likely to reduce significantly prospects for independence and self-support as an adult.

---

22. Autism Society of Michigan, *Newsletter*, March 2, 1994.

Family Support and Preservation

An important part of the rationale for providing cash support to families of children with significant disabilities is the fundamental principle of family support and preservation. SSI benefits help support the family itself so that it can provide a stable, nurturing environment in which the child is most able to develop and reach his or her full potential. The benefits undergird economic stability for poor families faced with the additional burden of caring for a disabled child.

Financial support that is available to two-parent families can ease some of the strains that lead to the higher risk of marital breakup among parents of children with disabilities. In all families, it assures parents that at least some of their other income will be available to meet the basic needs of the family.

Supporting families in their effort to care for their child at home is more efficient, cost-effective and humane than maintaining children in out-of-home settings. The cost of SSI benefits in support of families is far less than costs entailed in foster care, congregate arrangements or institutions. One study estimates the cost of out-of-home placement ranges from about $24,000 for specialized foster care to $95,000 in a state institution.[22] SSI benefits enable the best caregivers for children — their own families — to do so.

The Opportunity Costs of Care

The relatively sudden onset of a major disability in a child may wipe out the savings of a family of middle income and markedly diminish household income through the loss of wage earnings. A child with a disability often requires substantial in-home caretaking. Where two parents may have been employed prior to the onset of the disability, one may now need to remain at home or take a lower-paying position that allows for more flexibility in meeting unpredictable caretaking needs. Low-income families, given already marginal incomes, face a particular burden of foregone earnings while meeting the disability-related needs of their child.

Community Integration and Awareness

The benefits of keeping children with significant disabilities in the community go beyond the benefits to the individual child. Clearly, the child benefits by seeing and experiencing routine activities of daily living, whether it is getting on a school bus, going to the park, seeing other children and how they behave in public or maintaining significant personal relationships. The benefits are particularly important for children with mental impairments. Second, by living in the community, the child faces less of a transition upon reaching adulthood and entering the work force and establishing appropriate workplace relationships. Community integration also educates the community. It allows other children and adults who would otherwise have no direct experience with disabilities to look beyond an individual's particular impairments to see his or her abilities and individuality, and to become comfortable with having persons with disabilities as co-workers. In brief, community integration enhances acceptance of individuals with disabilities into the world of work.

Choice of Methods of Support

We considered a broad range of alternative approaches to support children with disabilities, such as vouchers for special services or block grants to states for services in lieu of cash.

Vouchers in Lieu of Cash Support. A voucher proposal might be viewed as a way to ensure that the assistance is used only for the child's benefit. For example, one might issue the family a voucher that could be used only for the disability-related needs for the child. We rejected the voucher idea as poorly suited to meeting the real needs of families with disabled children and as administratively very cumbersome and ill-fitted to the purpose of the SSI benefit.

As noted, the purpose of SSI benefits is not only to meet disability-related costs, but to help meet the opportunity costs of care and the child's basic needs for food, clothing and shelter. The opportunity costs parents face of foregoing paid employment in order to care for the child is a cost that cannot be met by vouchers. Furthermore, the disability-related needs of the child are extremely varied, and the vendors of those goods and services are just as diverse. Should specially-trained babysitters, clothing stores, vendors of diapers, transportation, toys, educational equipment, and providers of respite care be required to accept vouchers in lieu of cash for the goods and services they sell? Should contractors who adapt a child's home to accommodate a disability be paid vouchers? Should landlords accept vouchers as partial payment for rent? To administer such vouchers would be administratively awkward and expensive. Moreover, it would add an extraordinary intrusion of bureaucratic micro-management into decisions that can usually best be handled by families.

In those relatively rare instances where concern about parental misuse of funds or neglect of their children is warranted, child protective services should intervene, regardless of the source of the family's income.

Direct Services in Lieu of Cash Support. We considered whether direct services would be an appropriate substitute for cash support for families. The services needed by families are extremely diverse and vary widely in their availability in different localities. Service delivery may be effective in some communities, but less effective or nonexistent in others. One may need transportation services, but be required to schedule it a week in advance, or it may not be available at all. A respite care program could provide a caretaker, but that professional may be more expensive and less compatible than an experienced caretaker chosen by the family. A cash payment empowers families by giving them flexibility to purchase the goods and services that are appropriate to their own particular child's needs. And, as already noted, direct services do not compensate for the opportunity cost of care or help meet the child's basic needs of food, shelter and clothing.

The idea of substituting block grants to states for services, in lieu of federal cash support to families, has the appearance of decentralizing the locus of control from the federal to the state level. For meeting the needs of children with disabilities, however, the clearest decentralization of control is to place the purchasing power directly in the hands of families who care for the child.

Tailoring Benefit Amounts to Exact Needs. In theory, the idea of trying to match cash benefit amounts with the precise, demonstrated needs of children with disabilities has appeal. It would appear to target cash support where the need is greatest. The SSI payment, in contrast, is a form of "rough justice" that allocates cash support on established formulas based on the family's low income and the child's significant disability. After considering the implications of tailoring monthly cash support to precise needs, the method of "rough justice" has much to recommend it.

The administrative pitfalls of this approach are similar to those of vouchers or direct services as substitution for cash. It represents an extraordinary intrusion into family life because it would require frequent government assessment of each individual child's needs. It would entail far higher administrative costs, which would diminish the funds available for direct support to families. If such tailored support were designed to cover the true individualized costs of low-income disabled children and their families, the cost might easily exceed the cost of SSI.

In brief, we conclude:

There is a clear rationale and a compelling need for SSI cash support to families with a disabled child. The basic purpose of these benefits is to support and preserve the capacity of families to care for their disabled children in their own homes by:

- *Meeting some of the additional disability-related costs of raising a disabled child;*

- *Compensating for some of the income lost because of the everyday necessities of caring for a disabled child; and*

- *Meeting the child's basic needs for food, clothing and shelter.*

Without these supports, disabled children would be at a much greater risk of losing both a secure home environment and the opportunity for integration into community life, including the world of work.

Chapter 4

Benefits for Families With More Than One Eligible Child

We believe that SSI payments to families with more than one disabled child should be calibrated to recognize economies of scale in shared living arrangements. There is currently no such adjustment in the SSI benefit for children; each eligible child can receive up to the full federal benefit of $458. The absence of a family maximum permits unduly large benefits to be paid in those relatively rare cases of multi-beneficiary households.

We believe that a family maximum limit should apply to such households. For example, the benefits would be: a full benefit for a family with one child; 1.5 times the basic benefit for a family with two disabled children; and 2.0 times the basic benefit for families with three or more children with disabilities. These increments of 50 percent of the full benefit are about equivalent to the adjustments in the poverty threshold to take account of family size and the economies of scale from shared living arrangements. Such an adjustment is also consistent with other provisions of the SSI program, which pays 1.5 times the basic benefit to eligible married couples when both spouses meet the eligibility criteria as disabled, blind or aged individuals.

The large majority of children receiving SSI are the only beneficiary in the family. Of the households with a disabled child under 18 receiving SSI, 94 percent had only one disabled child, 5 percent had two children receiving SSI, and fewer than 1 percent had three or more children receiving SSI. These households include those with foster care children and adopted special-needs children.[23]

There should be an exception to the family maximum rule in certain circumstances. For example, families should be exempt from the rule if they have a child who would otherwise require institutional care for their disabilities (so-called "Katie Beckett" children who need round-the-clock nursing care). Exemptions from such a limit are also appropriate for foster care families who care for more than one disabled child or families who work through social service agencies to adopt special-needs children. Furthermore, the limit on cash benefits for families should not preclude Medicaid eligibility for any child in the family who meets the disability criteria of the SSI program. We recommend:

Benefits for families with more than one disabled child should be limited to 1.5 times the individual benefit for two children and 2.0

---

23. Social Security Administration, Office of Supplemental Security Income, *Study of SSI Recipients in Multi-Recipient Households*, March 1994; and Social Security Administration, Office of Supplemental Security Income. The Committee considered the family benefit adjustment only as it would apply to families with more than one disabled child. The status of parents, grandparents, or other relatives who receive SSI based on age or disability should be considered separately.

times the individual benefit for three or more children, with appropriate exceptions to those limits for "Katie Beckett" children (who require round-the-clock nursing care), foster care families and adopted special-needs children. No disabled child should lose Medicaid eligibility because of this limit on cash benefits for the family.

Chapter 5 Strengthening Eligibility Criteria

This chapter begins with a review of the changes in the composition of childhood benefit allowances after 1990 — particularly the growing number of allowances based on mental disorders other than mental retardation. We then consider allegations that parents "coach" their children to perform poorly in order to qualify for benefits and find no evidence to support such claims. Our recommendations to strengthen the eligibility criteria would improve the quality of decisions in several ways. They would avoid any perception that inappropriate behavior, in and of itself, is a basis for receiving benefits. Changes in the IFA would break its close tie with the mental disorders listings that cause it to be the basis for allowances mainly for mental disorders. Other recommendations would improve the quality of evidence for disability determinations and the quality of data for evaluating the nature of disabling conditions of children who receive SSI.

Changing Composition of New Entrants to the Childhood Disability Rolls

In 1990, the Supreme Court issued its decision in *Sullivan* v. *Zebley* and SSA's childhood mental disorders listings were updated. Since then, the most rapid growth in childhood claims and allowances has been for those based on mental disorders other than mental retardation. Mental retardation has remained the primary diagnosis for about 4 in 10 children on the SSI rolls (table A-1). Children with other mental disorders, in contrast, increased from 8 percent to 22 percent of children on the SSI rolls between 1990 and 1994, and they accounted for 31 percent of those newly allowed benefits in 1994 (table A-2). There is great diversity within that group. It includes children with severe mental illness, such as organic mental disorders, schizophrenia, mood disorders (including depression, manic and bipolar disorders), autism, anxiety-related disorders and other relatively rare mental illnesses. The most rapid growth in allowances, however, has been for children with ADHD as their primary diagnosis, which rose from 7 to 11 percent of allowances between 1992 and 1994. Children with behavioral disorders, such as personality disorders, conduct disorders and oppositional defiant disorders, accounted for about 5 percent of new allowances in 1994. Those with learning disorders, which were first coded separately in SSA's administrative data in February 1994, accounted for about 2 percent of allowances in calendar year 1994.

Over the past decade there has been growing recognition that certain childhood conditions — such as ADHD and learning disabilities — are, in fact, diagnosable disorders. In the past, their symptoms in children were more often viewed as carelessness, lack of motivation or misbehavior. As such conditions are increasingly recognized, they are found to be highly prevalent in the population and to have a broad spectrum of severity. In some cases they are genuinely disabling. The question for SSI policy is whether, and under what circumstances, they should be found so disabling as to qualify a child for SSI benefits.

Experts in ADHD estimate that its prevalence is much higher than most lay people realize. As many as 3 to 5 percent[24] of school-age children — or 1.4 to 2.4 million children[25] — are affected by the disorder. There is little agreement, however, regarding the rates of ADHD severe enough to create significant disability. Most authorities maintain that the large majority of children with ADHD do not have significant disability. By December 1994, about 60,000 children had entered the SSI rolls with ADHD as their primary diagnosis since that disorder was first coded separately in SSA's administrative data in 1991. Learning disorders also are extremely prevalent in the population. If almost all such children should not be considered so disabled as to receive SSI, SSA's criteria need to be very clear on how to distinguish only the severely disabling consequences of such conditions.

Little Evidence of "Coaching" or Inaccurate Allowances

We are mindful of concerns about motivational issues surrounding the payment of benefits based on mental disorders, where symptoms are largely behavioral in nature. Particularly troublesome are allegations that parents coach their children to misbehave or do poorly in school so that they can qualify for benefits.

In the childhood disability program today, evidence of such coaching or "gaming the system" is extraordinarily thin — and appears to be based on anecdotes or perceptions of dubious benefit claims, which upon investigation are found to have been denied.

Studies of allowances for children with ADHD or behavioral disorders by SSA,[26] the Office of Inspector General of the U.S. Department of Health and Human Services[27] and the U.S. General Accounting Office (GAO)[28] all have found scant evidence of coaching or malingering. Further, on claims where coaching was suspected, the benefit claim was usually denied. After completing its study, SSA took several actions: it clarified instructions to disability examiners; provided additional training to adjudicators on the issue of coaching and malingering; and set up an 800-number to receive anonymous reports of perceived coaching.[29] The number of cases reported to date on the toll-free line is small.

In brief, allegations of widespread abuse or inappropriate allowances have not been substantiated. Furthermore, data from administrative records show that children who receive SSI have very significant cognitive, physical or emotional disabilities. Mental retardation continues to be the most common primary diagnosis, with about half of all school-age children on the SSI rolls having that as their primary diagnosis (table A-1).

We believe our recommendations to strengthen the eligibility criteria will improve the process and will avoid any mistaken perception that inappropriate behavior, in and of itself, is a basis for allowing SSI benefits.

---

24. The 3-5 percent figures come from population surveys. N.M. Lambert, et al., "Prevalence of Hyperactivity in Elementary School Children as a Function of Social System Definers," *American Journal of Orthopsychiatry*, vol. 48, 1978, pp. 446-63; and P. Szatmari, et al., "Ontario Child Health Study: Prevalence of Attention Deficit Disorder with Hyperactivity," *Journal of Child Psychology and Psychiatry*, vol. 30, 1989a, pp. 219-30.
25. The numbers apply the 3-5 percent estimates to the population of children ages 5-17 in 1994, according to the U.S. Bureau of the Census.
26. Social Security Administration, *Findings from the Study of Title XVI Childhood Disability Claims*, May 1994.
27. U.S. Department of Health and Human Services, Office of Inspector General, *Concerns about the Participation of Children with Disabilities in the Supplemental Security Program*, A-03-94-02602, October 1994.
28. U.S. General Accounting Office, *Social Security: New Functional Assessment Process Results in Questionable Eligibility Decisions for Children*, February 1995.
29. Testimony by Dr. Shirley S. Chater, Commissioner of Social Security, before the Committee on Finance, U.S. Senate, March 22, 1995.

Recommendations to Strengthen the Functional Assessments

Functional assessment of disability strengthens and improves the determination of eligibility for SSI. Looking at medical diagnoses that exclude functional measures would include in SSI some children who are not severely disabled and exclude others who are. Indeed, for many childhood disorders, ability to function is a critical part of the medical diagnosis.

Nevertheless, functional assessment techniques are far from perfect. In particular, there is a potential problem with double counting, and functional assessments often use less that the best evidence. These problems can and should be remedied administratively.

After reviewing the composition of recent entrants to the childhood benefit rolls, evaluating the regulatory criteria for assessing childhood disability and consulting with experts on childhood mental disorders, we conclude that changes are needed in the functional assessment in the mental disorders listings; in the IFA that was implemented to comply with the Supreme Court's decision in *Sullivan* v. *Zebley*; and in the interaction between the two.

Our recommendation would require SSA to revise a portion of its regulations for assessing childhood disability and to apply the new criteria to all future claims. The changes, themselves, would not require Congress to amend the Social Security Act. Congress could, however, require and set a timetable for the regulatory change as a way to clarify its intent and SSA's authority to strengthen, and in some ways tighten, the eligibility criteria for future applicants.

Specifically, the recommendations would modify SSA's childhood mental disorder listings and the IFA to: 1) reduce the emphasis placed on behavioral manifestations of a child's condition; 2) increase use of standardized tests to assess the functional consequences of mental disorders; and 3) revamp the IFA to make it less closely linked to the functional assessment of mental disorders.

1. Eliminate maladaptive behavior as a separate domain in the functional assessment in the childhood mental disorders listings and the IFA.

Figure 5-1 illustrates the sequential process for evaluating childhood disability, which parallels the process for adults. (A more complete description of the decision process is in appendix B.) Our recommendation would modify the functional assessment of mental disorders, at step 3 of SSA's sequential process, and at the IFA in step 4.

In step 3, the claimant's impairment(s) are compared with the "medical listings" — 100 or so specific mental or physical conditions that are described in regulations. If the claimant's impairment matches the listed condition or is medically equivalent to a listed condition, benefits are allowed.

For mental disorders, the medical listings at step 3 include two parts. Paragraph A lists specific diagnostic criteria which differ for each condition, such as mental retardation, schizophrenia, organic mental disorders, and so on. The listed diagnostic criteria are used to establish the *presence* of the mental disorder. Paragraph B lists functional "domains" and criteria, which are used to establish the *severity* of the disorder.

Figure 5-2 illustrates the functional domains that are used in paragraph B of the mental disorders listings for children (column 2).

For children, the personal/behavioral domain has two components: activities of daily living and maladaptive behavior. There is a separate domain for social functioning, which covers relationships with parents, other adults and peers. While maladaptive behavior is a consequence of certain mental illnesses and some forms of mental retardation, such behavior, if present, is likely to markedly limit social functioning as well. Thus, there is a potential for

Figure 5-1. Sequential Process for Evaluating Childhood Disability

1. Are you working?
(Yes = Deny)

2. Do you have a severe impairment?
(No = Deny)
Compare to medical listings

Mental	Other
3a. **Meet** both diagnostic (A) and functional (B) criteria? (Yes = Allow)	3a. **Meet** medical criteria in the listings? (Yes = Allow)
3b. **Equal?** Meet (B) and some of (A)? (Yes = Allow)	3b. Medically **equal** medical listings? (Yes = Allow)

3c. **Functionally equal** medical listings?
(Yes = Allow)
Do individualized functional assessment (IFA)

4. Given the IFA, is impairment(s) of comparable severity
to that which would disable an adult?
(Yes = Allow; No = Deny)

---

double-counting functional deficits related to maladaptive behavior.[30]

We recommend that SSA revise its regulations concerning functional assessment in paragraph B of the mental disorders listings to eliminate the separate domain for maladaptive behavior or to combine it with the domain of social functioning. The domain of marked restriction in activities of daily living would remain. We are not recommending changes in the diagnostic criteria used in paragraph A of the childhood mental listings.

The IFA is the last step of disability determination for children who are not awarded benefits based on meeting or equaling the medical listings for either mental or physical impairments (figure 5-1). As shown in figure 5-2, the IFA includes the same functional domains used in the mental disorders listings. Our recommendation to eliminate maladaptive behavior as part of the personal/behavioral domain applies to the IFA as well as to paragraph B of the mental disorders listings.

We recognize that maladaptive behavior is a genuine attribute of severe mental retardation or mental illness for some individuals. We believe that children with severe mental disorders can and should still qualify based on other diagnostic and functional criteria. The changes we recommend should rule out any perception that inappropriate behavior, in and of itself, is a basis for disability benefits.

---

30. Experts in childhood mental disorders report that maladaptive behavior is not one of the key domains used to assess the functional consequences of childhood disability. Quantitative standardized tests are available to assess the disabling consequences of childhood mental disorders. The most common of these, the Vineland Scale, uses as the key functional domains: communication; social function; activities of daily living; and (for young children) motor functioning.

2. Increase the use of standardized tests to assess the functional consequences of mental disorders.

Quantitative, standardized tests are available to assess the disabling consequences of childhood mental disorders. The use of such tests should be encouraged both to diagnose and to assess the functional consequences of childhood mental disorders. They can improve the quality of evidence used to determine a claim. As under current regulations, when standardized tests of functioning are used, two standard deviations from the mean would be the measure of marked deficit, which means only the 2 percent with the most severe functional impairments would meet the level of disability specified in the regulations.

Such standardized tests could be used by mental health experts SSA pays to perform consultative exams of child applicants who lack medical records. Many of the standardized psychological tests for diagnostic and functional assessment can be administered by a trained lay interviewer who is not an M.D. or Ph.D. As with many tests used in physical examinations, the test can be administered by a trained technician, while relying on psychiatrists or clinical psychologists to interpret the test results.[31]

3. Revamp the IFA to assess children's overall disability using criteria that are not so similar to those used in the mental disorders listings and that are appropriate for children with physical impairments as well as for children who have both mental and physical impairments.

SSA should revise its regulations to make the IFA a comprehensive assessment of the disabling consequences of the child's impairment(s), one that is qualitatively different from the assessment used for mental disorders.

The structure of the IFA, illustrated in figure 5-2, is problematic for several reasons. First, the IFA uses essentially the same criteria for assessing function as the mental disorders listing, yet sets a lower threshold for a finding of disability. For example, even if our recommendation for eliminating maladaptive behavior were implemented, the domains for the mental disorders listings and the IFA would be nearly identical, as shown in figure 5-3.

The IFA is similar to the mental disorders listings, yet sets a lower threshold for allowance. For example, the mental disorders listings specify a finding of disability based on **marked** deficits in **two** of four domains, while the IFA allows a finding of disability based on **one marked** and **one moderate** deficit in essentially the same domains. The IFA also makes allowances based on three moderate deficits. Consequently, it is not surprising that the IFA is the basis for allowance mainly for children with mental disorders. In 1994, the IFA was the basis for allowance for 42 percent of children with mental disorders as their primary diagnosis and only 7 percent of children with physical disabilities (table A-3).[32]

A second problem with the IFA was highlighted by GAO: the difficulty of assessing "moderate" limitations in functional domains.[33] The term "moderate" covers a broad range of severity between "minimal" (or "mild") and "marked," and requires examiners to use a great deal of judgement in distinguishing the degree of moderate limitation that should contribute

---

31. Diagnostic tests mentioned by experts consulted by the Children's Committee include: the Diagnostic Interview Schedule for Children (DISC); the Diagnostic Interview of Children and Adolescents (DICA); and the Kids' Schizophrenia and Depression Schedule (K-SADS). Standardized tests of functioning include the Vineland Scale, the Child and Adolescent Functional Assessment Scale (CAFAS), and the Global Assessment Scale for Children (C-GAS). In addition, extensive psychological profiles have been developed to identify and assess the severity of ADHD.

32. It is possible that some children who are found disabled based on the IFA would meet the stricter test in the mental disorders listings. The disability examiners are given somewhat conflicting instructions. They are to follow the sequential process, applying the more strict test first and the less strict test second. Yet, they also are told not to waste time and resources collecting additional evidence if they have enough evidence to allow a valid claim. Consequently, some children might be allowed based on the IFA when more evidence would have shown they met the stricter test. It is neither logical nor administratively efficient to sequentially assess the same functional domains using first a strict, then a less strict, test for finding disability.

33. U.S. General Accounting Office, op. cit., footnote 28, p. 13.

Figure 5-2. SSA's Functional Assessment of the Severity of Disabling Conditions

CURRENT POLICY

Paragraph B of Adult Mental Disorders Listings	Paragraph B of Childhood Mental Disorders Listings Children age 3-18	Childhood Individualized Functional Asssessment (IFA)
The required level of severity is met with TWO of the following:	The required level of severity is met with TWO of the following:	"Guidelines" are ONE marked and ONE moderate limitation or THREE moderate limitations among:

1. Marked restriction in **activities of daily living**.
 	
2. Marked restriction in **social** functioning.
 	
3. Deficiencies of **concentration, persistence or pace** causing frequent failure to complete tasks.
 	
4. Repeated episodes of **decompensation** in work, or work-like settings.
	1. Marked impairment in age-appropriate **cognitive/communication** functioning.
	
	2. Marked impairment in age-appropriate **social** functioning.
	
	3. Marked impairment in **personal/behavior** functioning as evidence by:
	   a. Marked restriction in age-appropriate activities of daily living; or
	   b. Persistent **maladaptive behavior** destructive to self, others, animals or property.
	
	4. Deficiencies of **concentration, persistence or pace** which cause frequent failures to complete tasks.
		1. **Cognitive** function.
		
		2. **Communication** function.
		
		3. **Motor** function.
		
		4. **Social** function.
		
		5. **Personal/behavior** function
		  • activities of daily living
		  • maladaptive behavior.
		
		6. **Concentration, persistence or pace.**

to a finding of disability.[34] As noted earlier, for conditions with high prevalence in the population, a broad spectrum of severity, and low likelihood of being so disabling as to be a basis for SSI benefits — such as ADHD and certain learning disabilities — it is particularly important to have clear criteria for determining the severity of the disabling consequences of the condition. For example, deficiencies of concentration, persistence or pace — one of the functional domains — are characteristic of some learning disabilities and of ADHD across the spectrum of severity. Criteria must be very clear to distinguish only the severely disabling levels of such conditions.

---

34. Most of the functional domains are evaluated in terms of the severity of the deficit. In the domain of concentration, persistence and pace, the severity of the limitation is distinguished in terms of the frequency of the child's inability to perform age-appropriate tasks. A marked deficit in this domain is **frequent** inability to complete age-appropriate tasks in a timely manner. A moderate deficit in this domain is illustrated by example in the regulations as: **frequent** inability to complete age-appropriate **complex** tasks, and occasional inability to perform **simple** age-appropriate tasks.

The third problem with the IFA is that it may fail to identify disabling consequences of physical impairments or diseases, or combinations of physical and mental disorders, because it so closely parallels the functional assessment in the mental disorders listings.

This is not to say that the IFA should be scrapped. It is an important part of the determination for two reasons. First, because not all impairments are included in the listings, not having an IFA could discriminate against some children with very severe — but unlisted — impairments. Second, SSA regulations state that the medical listings are set at a **higher** threshold of disability than is required by the statute (although the listings for different body systems may vary in this regard).[35] To the extent that this is true, individuals whose impairments do not meet or equal the medical listings, but nonetheless have impairments that meet the statutory definition, would be wrongly denied benefits if there were not a final step in the process that determined whether they, in fact, met the statutory definition.

The current IFA should be replaced with a comprehensive assessment that is appropriate for children with physical impairments or illnesses as well as for children with mental disorders in combination with physical impairments. Appropriate criteria might

Figure 5-3: Comparison of Functional Domains

Mental disorders listings	Individualized functional assessment
Cognitive/communication	Cognitive Communication
Social functioning	Social functioning
Activities of daily living	Activities of daily living
Concentration, persistence or pace	Concentration, persistence or pace
	Motor functioning

include neurological, sensory, fine and gross motor functioning, stamina and endurance, medical fragility and vulnerability to disease, and need for special equipment in order to function, as well as appropriate measures of functional deficits imposed by mental impairments.

Caution Against Over-Reaction

We believe that new regulations should be developed expeditiously to strengthen childhood eligibility criteria and to apply them to all future benefit claims. At the same time, care should be taken to avoid radical shifts in adjudicative and legislative policy that have occurred in the past when steps were taken to strengthen eligibility criteria.

In its interim report, first issued in March 1994, the Panel recounted lessons learned from the tumultuous history of the Social Security disability programs.[36] Steps taken to strengthen eligibility criteria in the late 1970s escalated to radical retrenchment policies in the early 1980s and resulted in denying or terminating benefits on a large scale. The sharp cutback in eligibility brought widespread individual hardship and judicial challenges. States were at first reluctant, and then refused, to implement the harsh policies because it left them with the burden of care

---

35. Current SSA regulations state that the listings level of impairment represents a higher level of disability than that specified in the law. Current regulations for adults state that: a) meeting or equaling the medical listings is supposed to represent an impairment that precludes **any gainful** activity; while b) the assessment of residual functional capacity (RFC) for adults is supposed to reflect inability to engage in **any substantial gainful** activity, after taking into account the person's age, education, and prior work experience (as called for in the law). For children, a similar distinction is made: the statutory level of "comparable severity" is an impairment that **substantially limits** functioning "independently, appropriately, and effectively in an age-appropriate manner," while an impairment that meets or equals the listings is supposed to **preclude** that level of functioning.
36. Disability Policy Panel, *The Environment of Disability Income Policy: Programs, People, History and Context*, Interim Report, J.L. Mashaw and V.P. Reno (eds.) (Washington, DC: National Academy of Social Insurance, 1996).

for vulnerable populations whose federal benefits were denied or terminated. The policies were ultimately reversed.[37]

While we believe that eligibility criteria need to be strengthened, we also find that allegations of widespread inappropriate allowances are not substantiated and sharp cuts in the current rolls are not warranted.

Need for Longitudinal Evidence and Treatment Trials

Experts in childhood mental disorders report that accurate diagnosis of childhood mental disorders often requires a longitudinal medical and functional record, which applicants for SSI benefits may not have. A longitudinal medical and functional record can be of critical importance for diagnosing particular mental disorders, such as ADHD. In fact, many believe that a proper diagnosis of ADHD is not possible without a longitudinal record of six months or a year.[38]

Under current law,[39] SSA must develop a 12-month record in order to deny or terminate benefits. While the law does not require a 12-month record in order to allow benefits, as a practical matter, because it is not known in advance whether a claim will be allowed or denied, SSA instructs disability examiners to try to obtain a 12-month record in all cases.

Often, however, applicants do not have medical records for a 12-month period. In some cases they do not have any medical records. Children claiming SSI benefits are in very low-income families who may not have an ongoing relationship with a physician. If there is not sufficient evidence to determine whether the person has a "medically determinable impairment," the examiner arranges a consultative examination of the claimant by a psychiatrist or clinical psychologist, in the case of mental disorders, who is paid by SSA. For children, the examiner then seeks to obtain a longitudinal record of the functional consequences of a child's impairment from information provided by the family, school, neighbors or others who know the child.

In the consultative examination, the physician or psychologist may have little evidence to rely on other than the current report by the applicant. The evidence in such cases is much less than medical examiners want to rely on to reach a diagnosis, or even the lesser standard of finding a medically determinable impairment that is necessary to meet SSA's diagnostic criteria. If the consultative examiner concludes there is a medically determinable mental impairment, the evaluation proceeds to assess the child's functioning under paragraph B of the mental disorders listings and, if necessary, the IFA. If the consultative examiner concludes there is not a "medically determinable impairment," the claim must be denied. We believe that:

When a child's condition appears to meet the SSI criteria and longitudinal medical records are needed to confirm the diagnosis, but such records are lacking, a provisional benefit may be appropriate. During a period of, say, 12 months, SSI benefits and Medicaid would be provided on a provisional basis, with a review scheduled at the end of the period. The review at that time should be based on whether the child's condition meets the statutory definition of disability; that is, SSA would not be required to demonstrate that medical improvement has

---

37. Legislation in 1984 restricted the conditions under which benefits of those on the rolls could be terminated and required SSA to ease the overly restrictive eligibility criteria for persons with mental impairments. Other legislation enacted in 1989, while the *Zebley* case was being litigated before the Supreme Court, required that SSA engage in outreach activities to enroll eligible children in the SSI program.
38. The literature indicates that ADHD is marked by its early onset, that is, appearance of symptoms by the age of 7, and by its duration (it is not a transient disorder that disappears after a year or two — recent work suggests that ADHD continues well into adulthood for many). Therefore, a medical and behavioral history dating back to early childhood is very important for an accurate diagnosis. H.C. Parker, *Education Position Paper*, Children and Adults with Attention Deficit Disorder, January 1990.
39. Section 1614(a)(3)(G) of the Social Security Act.

occurred, as is now required in most reviews of continuing disability.

In some cases, a proper diagnosis of mental disorders in children may require that treatment be tried before assessing the long-term disabling consequences of childhood mental disorders. Experts who study and treat ADHD in children, for example, report that in many cases treatment can lead to substantially improved functioning of the child and that if treatment has not been tried, it should be sought before determining the long-term disabling consequences of particular mental disorders.[40] In light of these findings, we believe that:

Provisional benefits are also appropriate when medical evidence suggests that appropriate treatment would alleviate the disabling consequences of the child's condition. After the limited period, the review of the child's condition would be based on evidence that treatment had been tried and on the remaining functional consequences of the disorder.

If the disabling consequences of the child's condition are remedied by appropriate treatment, SSI benefits should end. If the diagnosis remains, but its disabling consequences were controlled by treatment, Medicaid should remain available to ensure continued access to the needed medical treatment.

Medicaid may be the only way low-income children gain access to needed health care. Children who receive SSI are automatically eligible for Medicaid in most states. Being found no longer disabled for purposes of SSI benefits should not cause loss of Medicaid coverage if that coverage is needed to ameliorate the disabling consequences of the child's conditions. Without continuation of Medicaid, there is a risk that SSI eligibility would resume in a short period.

---

40. Russell Barkley, Director of Psychology, Professor of Psychiatry, University of Massachusetts, and Secretary, Children and Adults with Attention Deficit Disorders.

Need for Better Diagnostic Data

Many of these recommendations are based on diagnostic data provided by SSA. These data provide only limited information regarding the clinical status of enrolled children. Insofar as data reported reflect only the primary diagnosis used to determine eligibility, it cannot be determined whether a given recipient has a simple disorder or has multiple associated conditions causing disability. For example, a child labeled with ADHD may have only ADHD or could have mental retardation, significant mobility impairment, and a seizure disorder as well.

Because there is significant co-morbidity in childhood disorders, particularly mental disorders, existing data on the "primary" diagnosis of children allowed benefits fails to convey the full nature of the child's impairments. In addition, there are concerns about the accuracy of SSA's procedures for recording diagnostic codes for primary, secondary and tertiary conditions among children. In the determination of disability based on mental disorders, diagnoses are of less importance than functional assessments. Consequently, the diagnostic coding of beneficiaries' conditions is not as good as it should be.

The accuracy and completeness of diagnostic codes is important for understanding and evaluating trends in the composition of the beneficiary population. Furthermore, to the extent that program records are used for referral of beneficiaries for appropriate services, accurate diagnostic codes supply key information to service providers. To improve research and evaluation of the SSI program and to improve linkage with treatment and services, we believe that:

Measures should be taken to ensure the accuracy of childhood disability primary and secondary diagnostic codes as well as outcomes of functional evaluations. These codes and indicators should be included on data files available for evaluating trends in the SSI program and its beneficiaries.

Chapter 6
Young Children: Links with Community-Based Services

While all children are expected to meet a high threshold of disability to qualify for SSI, there nonetheless is great diversity among young children in terms of the prospects for medical improvement or improved functioning. Young children with chronic health problems or disabilities need a wide range of therapeutic, educational and related services in order to enhance their chances for improved functioning. Their families, too, often require help in understanding and meeting their child's disability-related needs.

The Landscape of Service Programs

The services needed by families of children with disabilities are funded by a mix of federal, state and local funds. Federal laws provide some funding and set requirements or guidelines that states and localities must meet in order to qualify for federal funds. The services are administered at the state or local level, and they vary greatly in terms of who is eligible, what services are available and how families learn about them. The major programs under federal law are: a) Medicaid, which pays for health care services to low-income children with or without disabilities; b) the Maternal and Child Health program for children with special health care needs, which provides medical services to children with chronic illness or physical disabilities; c) special education programs in local school districts; d) Part H Early Intervention services for children from birth to age 3 who experience or are at risk of developmental delay; and d) grants to states to support planning and advocacy for children and adults with developmental disabilities. A brief overview of each follows.

Medicaid. The Medicaid program, authorized under title XIX of the Social Security Act, generally covers health and related services for children with disabilities who receive SSI. States may link eligibility for Medicaid with SSI in one of three ways. Medicaid eligibility may come automatically when the person becomes entitled to SSI. Thirty-two states and the District of Columbia follow this course. In other states, SSI recipients are eligible for Medicaid, but they have to file separately for it. Seven states use this method. Finally, so-called 209(b) states may use more stringent eligibility standards for Medicaid than for SSI. There are 12 209(b) states.

Medicaid's Early and Periodic Screening, Diagnosis and Treatment (EPSDT) program is of particular importance to children. Under EPSDT, states are required to provide a comprehensive physical evaluation and developmental screening as well as periodic vision, hearing, dental and general health checkups to all Medicaid-eligible children. Changes enacted in 1989[41] further provide that any physical or mental illness or condition that is identified

---
41. The Omnibus Budget Reconciliation Act of 1989.

during the EPSDT screens must be referred for treatment, and the treatment must be covered by Medicaid, even if those services would not normally be included in the state's Medicaid plan. In response to this change, some states have included in their Medicaid program: mental health services; occupational, physical, and speech therapy; private duty nursing; and nutrition services. In particular, the change opened up the possibility for Medicaid-covered services for mentally ill or developmentally disabled children. These and other Medicaid changes permit some services of public health departments, community health centers, school health services and programs for Children with Special Health Care Needs to be funded from Medicaid rather than earmarked grant funds.[42]

The EPSDT program is particularly important to children with disabilities in states that do not have comprehensive benefit coverage under the regular Medicaid program. The comprehensive service requirement also makes EPSDT potentially costly and administratively difficult for states. Many states are still struggling to get their EPSDT systems into full operation. Enormous variation exists among states in the details of the program that are left to states' discretion and in the percentage of the eligible population reached. Further, problems of access to health services remain for Medicaid-eligible children when pediatricians and other health care providers are not available or choose not to serve Medicaid patients because of low reimbursement rates, paperwork requirements or other burdens in complying with program requirements.

Maternal and Child Health. The Maternal and Child Health program, under title V of the Social Security Act, is required under the Children with Special Health Care Needs (CSHCN) program (formerly the "Crippled Children's Program") to provide habilitation and rehabilitation services to children receiving SSI. In the early years of the federal SSI program, there were earmarked appropriations and guidelines for the title V program specifically to serve disabled children receiving SSI. The earmarked funds were eliminated when the program was folded into the Maternal and Child Health Services block grant during the early 1980s.

States vary widely in the conditions they cover under CSHCN, the financial eligibility thresholds they impose, their administrative structures and their methods of either paying for or directly providing medical services. CSHCN services are available to families not covered by Medicaid, and the CSHCN program is designed to have Medicaid serve as first payer for Medicaid-eligible children. CSHCN tends to cover a relatively narrow range of medical conditions. Originally intended to assist children with polio and other conditions leading to orthopedic impairments, the program has gradually added more conditions, such as congenital heart problems, cystic fibrosis, and muscular dystrophy. However, CSHCN does not cover children whose principal disabling condition is mental retardation or mental illness.

Special Education. The federal Individuals with Disabilities Education Act (IDEA) authorizes grants to states for special education and, as a condition for receipt of federal funds, requires that states provide to all children with disabilities "free appropriate public education in the least restrictive environment." When a child has been found eligible for some type of special education, a special education teacher, in conjunction with the parents, develops an individualized education plan (IEP) for the child. The plan sets out a course of services the school will provide and annual education goals for the child. The IEP is revised each year.

While federal law mandates special education, federal funds account for only about 8 percent of special education expenditures, with approximately 55 percent coming from states and 37 percent

---

42. A. Evans and R.B. Friedland, *Financing and Delivery of Health Care for Children*, working paper, National Academy of Social Insurance, May 1994.

coming from local governments.[43] Because special education services are delivered in thousands of local school districts across the country, the extent of variation in those services is enormous. The variation reflects great disparities in financial capacities among school districts, and may also reflect differences in educational philosophy, availability of personnel, or the underlying attitude of school administrators and school boards toward the entire special education enterprise. Unlike Medicaid and SSI, there is no means test in determining a child's eligibility for special education services.

Federal law also requires that school districts must provide or pay for not only appropriate special education services, but also such "related services" as are necessary to assure that a child is able to learn effectively. Related services, which are received by a little over 20 percent of the special education population, include special transportation, physical, occupational or speech therapy, and evaluative or diagnostic medical services. These services can be costly, and school districts try to limit their expenditures for them or to have the assessment of need for these services be considered an EPSDT evaluation for Medicaid-eligible children, so that the federal/state Medicaid program is obligated to pay for them rather than the local school district.

Part H Early Intervention. The Part H Early Intervention program was added to the federal special education law in 1986 to extend to children from birth to age three a coordinated regime of medical, developmental, and social services to children experiencing developmental delays or at risk of experiencing such delays.

While some states sponsored forms of early intervention services prior to 1986, the aim of the federal legislation was to encourage all states to establish more extensive, coordinated systems of intervention. States were given five years to build up their systems in increments. Many, however, had difficulty meeting the deadline. Often states had problems establishing the necessary bureaucratic coordination among their own governmental agencies; or they couldn't find appropriate service providers in all areas of the state; or they had difficulty finding the money to fund a statewide system. In 1991, just before the five-year federal deadline ran out, Congress authorized two one-year extensions for states that had not met federal guidelines.

The Part H statute establishes a framework for eligibility rules but leaves the states considerable leeway in filling in the details. The statute sets out the three basic eligibility categories: exhibiting developmental delay; having a condition known to cause developmental delay; and at risk of developmental delay. States must cover children in the first two categories; the third is optional and few states have adopted it. Developmental delay is assessed in terms of level of functioning in five areas: cognitive; communicative; adaptive; social or emotional; and physical. The method of measuring functioning and the definition of the level necessary to qualify as a delay are left up to the states.

The law makes some services mandatory and leaves others optional. The core required services are physical, occupational and speech therapy, and service coordination. Medical services, except for consultations necessary to the provision of the other services, are not covered. The service coordination system is modeled after the special education process. The service coordinator, typically a social worker, nurse or early education specialist, works with the parents in establishing an individual family service plan (IFSP) that outlines a course of treatment for the next six months.

Under federal law, states are not allowed to charge parents for Part H services, but they are encouraged to draw on private insurance or Medicaid coverage of the families they serve. The law states that families cannot be denied access because of lack of insurance, and the federal share of Part H funds are to be the payer of last resort, after private insurance, Medicaid or other state or local funds.

---

43. Data are for the 1987-88 school year (the most recent year for which this breakdown is available). U.S. Department of Education, *Fourteenth Annual Report to Congress on the Implementation of the Individuals with Disabilities Education Act* (Washington, DC: U.S. Government Printing Office, 1992).

Administration on Developmental Disabilities.
The Administration on Developmental Disabilities of the U.S. Department of Health and Human Services funds four types of activities that are important for children or adults with disabilities. The Federal Developmental Disabilities Assistance and Bill of Rights Act defines developmental disability as: "a severe chronic disability which is attributable to a mental or physical impairment; is manifested before the age of 22; is likely to continue indefinitely; results in substantial functional limitations in three or more of the following areas of major life activity: 1) self-care; 2) receptive and expressive language; 3) learning; 4) mobility; 5) self-direction; 6) capacity for independent living; and 7) economic self-sufficiency and thus requires special services for an extended time."[44] The basic grants provide funds to states to support developmental disabilities planning councils. The councils, composed of public officials and private citizens, carry out general planning in the states for services to developmentally disabled adults and children, and they provide grants to local groups for innovative efforts in service delivery or research. The Protection and Advocacy programs fund offices in the states that provide legal assistance and consumer information to the developmentally disabled. University affiliated programs get funds from the Administration on Developmental Disabilities to support research; training for people who work with the disabled; and the design of assistive devices for persons with developmental disabilities. Finally, the Projects of National Significance provide discretionary funds for innovative demonstration projects around the country.

The Landscape from the Perspective of Families

While a broad range of federal laws and programs are designed to improve access to services needed by low-income children in general, or by children with disabilities in general, families of children with disabilities report great difficulty and frustration in their attempts to learn what is available and how to gain access to the services at the local level. Interviews with families of children with disabilities indicate that systems for providing assistance are often fragmented, confusing and difficult to access.[45] Field interviews in two localities (Connecticut and Virginia) with both middle-income and low-income parents reveal their great frustration in negotiating the system of services their children need:

- *In both Connecticut and Virginia, parents reported how the physical and emotional strain of caring for a young child with a disability was terribly aggravated by their feeling of stumbling in the dark as they tried to find sources of information and support. The mother of the baby with a chromosomal abnormality took her son to most of the leading medical facilities in the central part of Connecticut in search of a diagnosis. Yet once the diagnosis was established, she found herself having to rely on nothing but the phone book to locate the services her son needed.*

- *Another parent, whose first and third children had disabling conditions, only found out about SSI for her first child in the course of seeking help for her third — several years after her first child's diagnosis.*

- *Parents' difficulties in getting the information they need stem from many causes. Often the professionals one might expect to know about programs of assistance simply don't. A recent survey of Connecticut pediatricians, for example, found that only 24 percent of the respondents had heard of the Part H Early Intervention program.*[46]

- *The medical director of a major children's hospital in Richmond, himself the father of a child with a severe disability, confirmed that the situation is similar in Virginia.*

- *The head of pediatric social work at one of Connecticut's leading hospitals reported she had never heard of the Medicaid EPSDT program. The head of a state hotline for early intervention, herself*

---

44. 42 U.S.C. 6001.
45. Cedarbaum, op. cit., footnote 15, pp. 30-33.
46. Cedarbaum, op. cit., footnote 15, p. 32; and M.B. Bruder, "Survey of Connecticut Pediatricians on Early Intervention Services," unpublished paper, University of Connecticut Health Center, 1993, pp. 7-8.

the mother of a disabled child, who had set up the hotline because of the difficulties she faced getting information for her daughter, reported she was not surprised. "No one knows about EPSDT," she explained. Many parents reported they had learned most of what they needed to know once they found a "veteran" group of parents of children with disabilities they could consult.

Recommendations

Families need help to negotiate the complex and fragmented systems that are designed to serve children with disabilities. Parents from all walks of life — including those who are highly educated and sophisticated advocates for their child's welfare — report great barriers to gaining access to the services their disabled children need. For low-income parents, regardless of educational level, the need for help in gaining needed services is particularly acute.

We recognize that while the local Social Security office is the initial contact for gaining access to SSI benefits, those offices have neither the staff resources nor the expertise to help provide the individualized help that families need to negotiate the complex system of services. Two kinds of improvements are needed. One is better information and referral when families apply for SSI benefits for their children; the other is individualized care coordination services, which some families may need.

Information and Referral. Information and referral can be done in two ways: by providing information directly to SSI applicants or beneficiary families, or by referring information in case files to local service agencies that are responsible for serving low-income children with disabilities.

SSA's local district offices would seem to be an opportune locale for families to get information about programs and services their children may need. The local district office is where families initially apply for benefits and where SSI beneficiaries have periodic recertification of eligibility under the SSI income and resources test. We believe that:

SSI cash assistance for infants and young children should be coordinated with the services they and their families need to enhance the child's prospects for healthy development. If SSA is not equipped to provide information about local programs, that information and referral role should be filled under contract with private or other public agencies. Such organizations could assemble user-friendly information about local or national service networks available to families of children with different types of disabilities. SSA would be responsible for having the informational materials available in its local district offices, but questions would be referred to the contractor who assembled the information.

Various parent groups around the country could be among possible contractors, such as the Federation of Children with Special Needs or Parent Training and Information Centers, which are funded by the U.S. Office of Special Education Programs to provide technical assistance to families of children with disabilities. SSA's disability determination services (DDSs) are a potential source for the referral of case files to other state or local agencies that serve children with disabilities. The DDS is a state agency that works under contract with SSA to make the medical determination of whether children or adults meet the test of disability for receiving SSI or Social Security benefits. DDSs are organized in varying ways in different states. In some states they are part of the rehabilitation agency. In others they are part of welfare or social service departments, and in others they are located in education departments or labor departments. Applicants for benefits typically do not visit the DDS. The DDS does, however, assemble the applicant's medical records and, for children, it assembles records from schools and other sources. The DDS could serve a referral role, by sending information about children in need of services to the state or local agency that has responsibility for providing services appropriate to the child's needs.

Individualized Care Coordination. Ideally, local service agencies would be responsible for coordinating care for children receiving SSI and their families, using the special education model of an individualized educational plan that sets goals and allocates responsibility for their achievement to specific participants and services providers.

The diversity of clinical problems affecting children with disabilities would require allocating the care coordination role among agencies. For example, the Maternal and Child Health programs, especially in the stronger states, could play an active role in assuring the coordination of services for children with physical, and to a degree developmental, disabilities. Yet they have little expertise in mental illness or mental retardation. Children with mental impairments would require a different agency. It is unclear whether state or local mental health agencies which serve adults with severe mental illness are equipped to meet the needs of children. Responsibility for service coordination for children with mental retardation could be placed in the public school system, the state education agency, or the agency serving people with developmental disabilities. We believe that:

States and localities should be encouraged to develop a working consortium among the agencies serving children with disabilities, with clear allocation of responsibility for service coordination for specific categories of children receiving SSI. They should coordinate with parent groups, the state agency that evaluates disability and SSA field offices, as appropriate.

Ongoing Assessment and Tracking. We believe that SSA should target for continuing disability reviews (CDRs) young children who have the best prospects of medical and functional improvement. For example, many very young children who qualify for benefits based on low birth weight should show substantial gains in development when reassessed at age one or two. Although a few conditions may be very disabling (such as multiple congenital anomalies or major central nervous system malformations), the large majority of very small infants merit CDRs. SSA's recent initiative to conduct CDRs for children allowed because of low birth weight and other disorders should be continued. CDRs might also target other types of childhood impairments that have good prospects for medical improvement as the child matures. We believe that:

Children's progress should be tracked and periodically reviewed to ensure that those who recover do not remain on the SSI disability rolls and that those whose disabilities persist are linked to services appropriate to their changing needs as they grow older.

The purpose of ongoing reassessment of a child's condition is not solely to determine whether medical recovery has occurred. It should also reassess the basis for the child's continuing eligibility, as children's conditions and diagnoses may change as they grow older.

If, as recommended above, SSA district offices and the DDSs had mechanisms for providing information and referral for community-based services, the child's disability review would be an opportunity to update the referral for community-based services as the child grows older.

Medicaid Coverage and CDRs. Under current policy, when children are found no longer disabled as a result of a CDR, their SSI benefits end. Continued eligibility for Medicaid would then depend on rules that vary widely from state to state regarding Medicaid coverage for children who are not eligible for SSI.[47] We believe that Medicaid coverage should

---

47. Under federal law, effective April 1990, states are required to cover under Medicaid all children under age six whose income is below 133 percent of the federal poverty level. Further, since July 1, 1991, states are required to cover children under age 19 who were born after September 30, 1983, and whose family income is below 100 percent of the federal poverty level. Consequently, coverage of all children through age 18 with incomes below the poverty threshold will take effect in 2002. States are permitted, but not required, to cover pregnant women and infants under one year old with incomes below a state maximum that is more than 133 percent of the poverty threshold, but not more than 185 percent. As of July 1993, 34 states had made use of this option to cover pregnant women and infants; 25 had set their income limits at the maximum of 185 percent.

be continued for children who leave the SSI rolls if their diagnostic condition remains and Medicaid coverage is needed to control or ameliorate the disabling consequences of their condition. That is:

Children who leave the SSI rolls because the disabling consequences of their conditions are ameliorated or controlled by proper treatment should continue to have Medicaid coverage to continue their treatment.

Chapter 7 Transition to Adulthood

We believe that it is essential to develop policies that assist in channelling teenagers who receive SSI into a "work track" as they enter adulthood, rather than looking forward to a lifetime on cash benefits. We also recognize that for some children with very significant cognitive disability or multiple disabilities, maximum functioning and independence does not include competitive employment. For others, success in a work track may not necessarily mean they will completely leave the SSI rolls. Among teenagers receiving SSI, over half (54 percent) have mental retardation as their primary diagnosis. Appropriate education and training can improve their chances to work and live as independently as possible. Some may work in competitive or supported employment, but some who work may still need to rely on the SSI cash safety net and its section 1619 work incentive provisions in their adult years.

For other children, particularly those with primarily physical or sensory impairments, the support provided by SSI, in conjunction with appropriate education, habilitation, adaptive equipment and services, should enable many to become self-supporting and ultimately leave the benefit rolls.

The Young Adults' Perspective

The focus groups conducted for the Panel reveal the extraordinary diversity of those entering adulthood with significant disabilities. Both young people with disabilities and parents of children who are severely impaired participated in the focus groups and were interviewed. The parents, without exception, wanted their profoundly disabled children to be treated with love and respect, and to be given the maximum responsibility and independence possible. In some cases, that meant having those who care for their adult children understand their nonverbal signals about what they want or need. In some cases, parents considered part-time sheltered work as an option. The parents were very concerned about the quality of care available to their children and were deeply concerned about who would fill the caregiver role if their child should outlive them.

The young adults who participated in the focus groups were able to speak for themselves and get to the focus group site. They, too, showed great diversity in the nature of their disabilities, their outlook on life, their accomplishments, aspirations and adjustment to their disabilities. Some of the young adults on SSI were successfully making the transition to work.

- *Two participants who described themselves as "retarded" or "slow to learn" had established themselves in stable living arrangements and had part-time jobs. One had received a large lump-sum payment, probably a Zebley retroactive award, that he and his mother had used to help pay for their small house. The second young man appeared to have entered the SSI rolls at age 18. Both had long-term relationships with social service networks. A social worker or skills-trainer helped them through difficulties with their jobs, living arrangements, budgets or other coping situations. They seemed unconcerned about SSI benefit rules and counted on their case workers to deal with SSA and keep their records straight. Their aspirations were to "be around good people, have a safe place to live," and they were proud of their accomplishments at work "helping people find things in the store" or "carrying groceries for little old ladies."*

Other young adults rely on SSI as temporary support while they pursue post-secondary education and look forward to successful professional careers completely off the SSI rolls.

- *A young man who was blind was interviewed by telephone. He was attending college with tuition support from the State Commission for the Blind. He was extremely upbeat, planned to get married soon and looked forward to a successful career as a special education teacher. He had been contacted by the State Commission when he reached age 18 about his potential eligibility for SSI. He qualified quickly and is grateful for the support while he pursues his education.*

Still other young adults with lifelong disabilities lacked these kinds of stable supports. They had aspirations for work careers, but their connection with special education had been sporadic and disrupted.

- *A young man in Iowa, age 24, reported he had a stroke at birth and, because he was paralyzed on one side, did not walk until he was six. When he was about 10, he started having seizures for which he continues to take medication. He had been denied SSI when his family lived in another state because his parents made too much money in the steel mills. He fondly recalls a teacher at the "handicapped school" there who helped boost his horizons and build confidence that he could do whatever he set out to do. He left that school because his family moved to Texas to find work. There he attended regular high school. But when he had seizures in class, they thought he was asleep and dropped him from school,*

for which he was punished by his step-father. His SSI benefits are a source of security and he was reluctant to risk them. He has yet to obtain his general equivalency diploma (GED), but wants to have a career in art work or architectural drawing. He did not know how to go about it or where to turn to find the information he needed.

Still other young adults had disabilities with recent onset. Their disabilities had brought radical changes in their lives.

- *A young man, age 18, who had partial blindness and recurring headaches from a shooting accident when he was 16, got on SSI to help pay the hospital bills. He spoke hesitantly about being treated as "different" from other people or from the way he used to be. "It is easier," he said, "when you realize that people just want to know how you are doing. They don't think less of you." He was attending the local community college working toward his GED, although doing all the reading was difficult. He believes he can do a job, and hopes that his family will help him find work when he has finished his schooling.*

The varied experience of the young adults reveal both the potential for success and existing gaps in supports for children and teenagers with disabilities. Building on existing special education and transition planning requirements holds promise for children who go through the special education system. Those who fall through the cracks in that system, or who acquire disabilities as they become adults, require supports beyond the public school system.

Transition Planning and Benefit Security for Teens

We believe that programs in high school should prepare teenagers and young adults with significant disabilities for productive employment to the maximum extent possible. For children who have grown up with disabilities, transition planning and modifications in SSI policy to encourage such planning should be made when children reach adolescence.

Under IDEA, the federal government mandated in 1990 for the first time that all students in special education programs receive transition services by the age of 16. Under that law, the individualized education plan for special education students must include a statement of the needed transition services for students beginning no later than age 16 and annually thereafter (and, when appropriate, beginning at age 14 or younger), including a statement of the interagency responsibilities or linkages (or both) before the student leaves school.[48]

Transition services are defined in IDEA as a coordinated set of activities for a student, designed with an outcome-oriented process, which promotes movement from school to post-school activities, including post-secondary education, vocational training, integrated employment (including supported employment), continuing and adult education, adult services, independent living or community participation. The coordinated set of activities is to be based on the individual student's needs, taking into account his or her preferences and interests, and includes instruction, community experiences, the development of employment and other post-school adult living objectives, and, when appropriate, acquisition of daily living skills and functional vocational evaluation.[49] It is not yet clear what impact the new requirement for transition planning has had on post-secondary school outcomes for youths with disabilities.

New SSI legislation enacted in 1994 requires a reassessment of children's disability status (a CDR) when they reach age 18. The law requires that the reassessment use adult disability criteria, and if the child's disability does not meet those criteria, benefits would end. The new law applies to beneficiaries who turn 18 in May 1995 or later and requires that SSA conduct the CDRs for at least one-third of such SSI recipients in each year, 1996 through 1998. SSA is to report to Congress on this activity by October 1, 1998.

---

48. 20 U.S.C. 1401(a)(1)(D).
49. 20 U.S.C. 1401(a)(20).

We believe that SSI policy should be modified to encourage teenagers to prepare for the world of work and that transition planning should provide clear information to the child and parents about SSI rules. The following proposal builds on the special education requirements for transition planning.

At age 14, teenagers on SSI, together with their parents and special education advisors, should begin setting career goals and developing transition plans. The plan would set a track for the child's educational goals for the remainder of secondary school and should include: (1) academic preparation for attending college; or (2) vocational preparation that includes survey courses as well as concentration in the target vocational goal; and (3) preparation for life skills and independent living as adults.

Those involved in counseling young people in vocational planning should consult with local employers to understand their needs and hiring decisions. Vocational education should include opportunities for vocational training on the job as well as in the classroom.

Transition planning during the years between ages 14 and 18 should also provide information about SSI work incentives which can be used to pursue vocational goals after high school.

Transition planning for students receiving SSI should explain the current requirement that young people receiving SSI will have a CDR, subject to the adult disability criteria, when they reach age 18. Information about the implications of that review should be explained to the child and the parents.

While they are pursuing their plans for work or further education after high school, youths between ages 14 and 18 on SSI should have assurance of benefit security until they reach age 18, even if they begin to demonstrate work skills.

In effect, during the transition period, youths engaged in a transition plan would be assured that their SSI benefits would not be at risk if they began to work in part-time jobs or demonstrated the capacity to work. Such a policy would assure teens and their parents that benefits would not be jeopardized by positive school achievements and/or work efforts. Because SSA is not currently doing CDRs on teenagers under age 18, this policy might have no added benefit cost, and could have some positive pay-off in terms of alleviating families' concerns and encouraging a work track for teenagers.

Appendix A Tables

Table A-1. Blind and Disabled Children Receiving SSI

Number and Percent Distribution by Primary Diagnostic Group, December 1988-1994

Diagnosis group	1988	1989	1990	1991	1992	1993	1994
Total	**298,300**	**299,200**	**338,200**	**426,600**	**618,700**	**769,700**	**889,700**
Diagnosis available	260,300	262,300	296,700	376,300	559,700	704,500	812,400
Percent distribution by primary diagnosis							
Total percent	**100.0**	**100.0**	**100.0**	**100.0**	**100.0**	**100.0**	**100.0**
Physical	51.8	51.7	51.0	47.4	42.7	40.7	38.8
Mental retardation	41.7	42.0	41.1	40.6	41.4	39.9	39.1
Other mental disorders	6.5	6.3	8.0	11.9	15.9	19.3	22.1
Number receiving SSI by primary diagnosis							
Physical	134,900	135,500	151,300	178,700	238,900	286,900	315,100
Mental retardation	108,600	110,200	121,800	152,700	231,600	281,400	317,400
Other mental disorders	16,800	16,600	23,600	44,900	88,900	135,200	179,900

Abbreviation: SSI = Supplemental Security Income.
Sources: Social Security Administration, *Annual Statistical Supplement to the Social Security Bulletin* (Washington, DC: U.S. Government Printing Office, selected years); and Social Security Administration, Office of Research and Statistics.

Table A-2. Entrants to the SSI Childhood Disability Rolls, 1992-1994

Percent Distribution by Detailed Mental Disorders Codes
(Initial DDS Allowances on Childhood Initial Claims)

Code	Disorder	1992	1993	1994[a]
Total	**Total initial allowances**	196,036	218,502	183,263
	Total with diagnostic codes	195,808	218,324	183,112
	Total percent	100.0	100.0	100.0
Total	Physical (nonmental) disorders	37.1	34.7	31.5
Total	Mental disorders	62.9	65.3	68.5
	Mental disorders by specific codes			
3180	Mental retardation	39.1	38.9	37.0
Total	**Mental disorders other than mental retardation**	23.8	26.4	31.5
Total	Learning and communication disorders	–[b]	–[b]	3.0
3152	Learning disorder (child)	–[b]	–[b]	1.8
3152	Speech and language delays (child)	–[b]	–[b]	1.2
Total	ADHD and behavioral disorders	11.8	14.4	16.6
3140	Attention deficit hyperactivity disorder	6.9	9.2	11.3
Total	Behavioral disorders	5.0	5.1	5.3
3010	Personality disorders	5.0	5.1	3.2
3120	Conduct disorders (child)	–[b]	–[b]	1.1
3138	Oppositional defiant disorder (child)	–[b]	–[b]	1.0
Total	All other mental disorders	11.8	12.2	11.9
2940	Organic mental disorders	2.0	2.1	2.0
2950	Schizophrenic / paranoid functional disorders	0.7	0.7	0.8
2960	Mood disorders (children)	2.9	3.2	3.5
2990	Developmental disability including autism	1.9	2.0	2.2
3000	Anxiety-related disorders	2.2	1.9	1.4
3030	Substance dependency — alcohol (child)	0.1	0.1	0.1
3040	Substance dependency — drug (child)	–[c]	0.1	0.1
3060	Somatoform disorders	–[c]	–[c]	–[c]
3070	Eating and tic disorders	0.2	0.1	0.1
3150	Developmental emotional disorder (infant)	1.7	2.1	1.8

a. 1994 data are through November 28, 1994 and are estimated by multiplying by 12/11.
b. These conditions were first coded separately in February, 1994.
c. Fewer than one-half of 1 percent.
Abbreviations: ADHD = attention deficit hyperactivity disorder, DDS = disability determination service, SSI = Supplemental Security Income.
Source: Social Security Administration, Office of Disability.

Table A-3. Basis for Allowance of Childhood Disability Claims by Detailed Mental Diagnostic Codes, 1994[a]

Percent distribution by basis for allowance

Code	Disorder	Total Number	Total Percent	Meets	Medically equals	Functionally equals	IFA
Total	Total initial allowances	167,991	100				
Total	Physical (nonmental) disorders	52,960	100	53	16	24	7
Total	Mental disorders	115,031	100	51	5	2	42
Mental disorders by specific codes							
3180	Mental retardation	62,188	100	63	2	1	32
Total	Mental disorders other than mental retardation	457	100	39	7	3	52
Total	Learning / communication disorders						
3152	Learning disorder (child)	2,941	100	8	2	2	88
3152	Speech and language delays (child)	2,075	100	8	12	12	67
Total	ADHD and behavioral disorders						
3140	Attention deficit hyperactivity disorder	18,934	100	35	3	1	61
Total	Behavioral disorders						
3010	Personality disorders	5,372	100	48	7	2	43
3120	Conduct disorders (child)	1,771	100	28	7	2	63
3138	Oppositional defiant disorder (child)	1,715	100	26	9	1	64
Total	Mental disorders other than mental retardation						
2940	Organic mental disorders	3,276	100	56	7	4	33
2950	Schizophrenic/paranoid functional disorders	1,380	100	65	6	2	28
2960	Mood disorders (children)	5,901	100	42	5	2	51
2990	Develop. disability including autism	3,666	100	66	6	2	26
3000	Anxiety-related disorders	2,340	100	36	6	2	56
3150	Developmental/emotional disorders (infant)	3,015	100	31	8	7	53

a. 1994 data are through November 28, 1994.
Abbreviations: IFA = individualized functional assessment, ADHD = attention deficit hyperactivity disorder.
Source: Social Security Administration, Office of Disability.

Appendix B Sequential Disability Determination for Adults and Children

Figure B-1 illustrates the sequential process for adults, and the process for children before the *Zebley* decision and after both the *Zebley* decision and the new mental disorders listings were implemented in regulations. Each step of the sequential process is meant to either render a decision to allow or deny benefits, or to move to the next step to further evaluate the nature and consequences of the claimant's disability.

Steps 1 and 2. Step 1 (Are you working?)[50] and step 2 (Do you have a severe impairment?) are used to deny claims for both adults and children. Their purpose is to limit the administrative cost to the government and the burden on private providers of medical and other evidence in cases where the claim would not be allowed.

Step 3 for adults. Step 3 is used to allow benefits for children or adults whose impairments can be *presumed* to be disabling. The 100 or so impairments or medical conditions that are in the medical listings are presumed to make an adult unable to work, and for a child, should be of comparable severity to those for adults. If an adult's impairment meets or equals the listed condition, benefits are allowed without further assessment of whether the impairment, in fact, makes him or her unable to engage in past work or any other work.

In figure B-1, the medical listings for mental disorders are shown separately to illustrate where the functional assessment in paragraph B of those listings fits into the sequential process. The mental disorders listings are made up of a capsule definition of the disorder as well as diagnostic criteria (in paragraph A) and functional criteria (in paragraph B). The diagnostic criteria are used to determine the *presence* of a mental disorder.[51] The functional criteria in paragraph B are used to determine the *severity of disability*, based on the mental disorder.

All claims based on mental disorders have a functional assessment (paragraph B) as part of the determination of whether the person's condition meets or equals the medical listings. In general, the condition **meets** the listings if both the diagnostic criteria in paragraph A and the functional criteria in paragraph B as well as the capsule definition of the disorder are met. The condition can **equal** the listings if the functional criteria are met, but only part of the diagnostic criteria are met.

---

50. In the law, work is defined as engaging in substantial gainful activity (SGA), which is defined in regulations as earning $500 a month or more for people who are not blind.

51. The diagnostic criteria in paragraph A are based on the Diagnostic and Statistical Manual (DSM) compiled by the American Psychiatric Association. It is the official classification of mental disorders that is used for diagnosis, treatment and epidemiological research on mental illness in the United States. The DSM is updated periodically. SSA's updates of the mental disorders listings for both adults and children in the 1980s were based on DSM-III. DSM-IV was issued in 1994.

Steps 4 and 5 for adults. In step 4, adults who are not presumed to be disabled based on having an impairment that meets or equals the medical listings have an assessment of their residual functional capacity (RFC) to determine the kinds of activities they can or cannot do. Their RFC is then compared with the duties required of their past work. If they are found able to do their past work, the claim is denied. If not, at step 5 their RFC and their age, education and work experience are taken into account to determine whether they can do other work that exists in the national economy. If so, the claim is denied. If not, the claim is allowed.

Step 3 for children — before Zebley. Before the *Zebley* decision, the sequential evaluation for children stopped at step 3, and was based solely on whether the child's impairment met or equaled one of those contained in the medical listings, as illustrated in the second column of figure B-1.

Step 3 for children — after Zebley. The Supreme Court found that basing childhood disability definitions solely on the medical listings did not satisfy the statutory definition of childhood disability as an impairment of "comparable severity" to that which would make an adult disabled. The Court required that an individualized functional assessment (IFA), comparable to the RFC for adults, be part of the disability evaluation for children.

The last column of figure B-1 shows the sequential process for children after the Court's decision was implemented in regulations in February 1991. This process also reflects changes that were made in December of 1990 when the childhood mental disorders listings were updated to use a two-part diagnostic and functional assessment comparable to that put in place for adults in 1985.

Regulations implementing the *Zebley* decision clarified step 3b for determining medical equivalence to the listings[52] and added step 3c — the concept of "functional equivalence" to the medical listings — and step 4, which provides an IFA comparable to the RFC for adults.

Step 3c — functional equivalence for children. In step 3c, which applies only to children, a child's impairment that does not meet or medically equal a condition on the medical listings can be found "functionally equivalent" to the listings. Functional equivalence is found if the overall functional limitations from the child's impairment, or combination of impairments, are equivalent to the limitations imposed by any listed impairment. The focus is on the disabling consequences of the child's medically determinable impairment(s).[53]

The regulations on "functional equivalence" to the medical listings also give examples of impairments that can be considered functionally equivalent to the listings. The examples are not meant to be exhaustive and include such conditions as: need for major organ transplant; very low birth weight; life-threatening major congenital organ dysfunction requiring surgical correction in the first year of life; any impairment causing marked restriction of both age-appropriate activities of daily living and social functioning; or the need for 24-hour supervision for medical or behavioral reasons.

Step 4 for children — the IFA. The IFA is the last step in the sequential process for children. It is meant to be the childhood equivalent of the RFC assessment for adults and is described further in the discussion of the proposal to strengthen it.

---

52. The current regulations state the following criteria for finding a child's impairment to medically equal the listings. "(1) If you have an impairment that *is* described in the [listings], but: (i) You do not exhibit one or more of the medical findings specified in the particular listing, or (ii) You exhibit all of the medical findings, but one or more of the findings is not as severe as specified in the listing, we will nevertheless find that your impairment is equivalent to that listing if you have other medical findings related to your impairment that are at least of equal medical significance. (2) If you have an impairment that *is not* described in the ... listings, or you have a combination of impairments, no one of which meets or is equivalent to a listing, we will compare your medical findings with those for closely analogous listed impairments. If the findings associated with your impairment(s) are at least of equal medical significance to those of a listed impairment, we will find that your impairment(s) is equivalent to the analogous listing." 20 CFR 416.926a (emphasis added).

53. 20 CFR 416.926a.

Figure B-1. Sequential Disability Determination Process

Adults	Children: Pre-Zebley	Children: Post-Zebley
1. Are you working? (Yes = Deny)	1. Are you working? (Yes = Deny)	1. Are you working? (Yes = Deny)
2. Do you have a severe impairment? (No = Deny)		2. Do you have a severe impairment? (No = Deny)
Compare impairment to medical listings	*Compare impairment to medical listings*	*Compare impairment to medical listings*

Adults		Children: Pre-Zebley	Children: Post-Zebley	
Mental	Other		Mental[b]	Other
3a. **Meet** both diagnostic (A) and functional (B) criteria? (Yes = Allow)	3a. Meet criteria in medical listings? (Yes = Allow)	3a. Meet criteria in medical listings? (Yes = Allow)	3a. **Meet** both diagnostic (A) and functional (B) criteria? (Yes = Allow)	3a. Meet criteria in medical listings? (Yes = Allow)
3b. Equal? Meet (B) and some of (A) (Yes = Allow)	3b. Medically equal medical listings? (Yes = Allow)	3b. Medically equal medical listings?[a] (Yes = Allow)	3b. Equal? Meet (B) and some of (A) (Yes = Allow)	3b. Medically equal medical listings? (Yes = Allow)

For Adults:

Assess residual functional capacity (RFC)

4. Can you do past work? (Yes = Deny)

Consider age, education and work experience

5. Can you do any other work? (No = Allow; Yes = Deny)

For Children: Post-Zebley:

3c. **Functionally equal** medical listings? (Yes = Allow)

Do individualized functional assessment

4. Given IFA, is impairment(s) of comparable severity to that which would disable an adult? (Yes = Allow; No = Deny)

a. Before 1990, SSA policy in Social Security Ruling 83-19 explicitly prohibited using an overall functional assessment to find that a claimant's impairment **equalled** the medical listings. A claimant with multiple impairments could meet or equal the listings only if at least one impairment, alone, met or medically equalled a specified listing.
b. The childhood mental disorders listings were modified in 1990 to include functional criteria similar to those put in the adult listings in 1985.
Abbreviation: IFA = individualized functional assessment.

Disability Policy Panel Biographies

Jerry L. Mashaw, Chair, is Sterling Professor of Law at Yale Law School and a Professor at the Institute of Social Policy Studies at Yale University. He is a leading scholar in administrative law and has written widely on social insurance and social welfare issues, including disability policy. His works related to disability policy include: *Social Security Hearings and Appeals* (1978); *Bureaucratic Justice: Managing Social Security Disability Claims* (1983); *Social Security: Beyond the Rhetoric of Crisis* (1988); and *America's Misunderstood Welfare State* (1990). He received his LL.B. from Tulane University and his Ph.D. in European governmental studies from the University of Edinburgh.

Monroe Berkowitz is Professor of Economics, Emeritus at Rutgers University and Director of Disability and Health Economics in the Bureau of Economic Research. He is also the Director of Research at Rehabilitation International. He is a leading authority on the economics of disability and rehabilitation in both public programs (Social Security disability insurance and workers' compensation), private disability insurance and public and private rehabilitation systems. Professor Berkowitz has also conducted extensive comparative analyses of foreign systems. His publications include: *Disability and the Labor Market* (1986), winner of the Book of the Year Award from the President's Committee on the Employment of People with Disabilities; and *Measuring the Efficiency of Public Programs,* (1988). He received his Ph.D. in economics from Columbia University.

Richard V. Burkhauser is a Professor of Economics and Associate Director for the Aging Studies Program at the Center for Policy Research, part of the Maxwell School of Citizenship and Public Affairs, at Syracuse University. He has published widely on social insurance issues, particularly in disability policy. He has also conducted several comparative analyses of foreign systems. His works include: *Disability and Work: The Economics of American Policy* (1982); *Public Policy Toward Disabled Workers: A Cross-National Analysis of Economic Impacts* (1984) and *Passing the Torch: The Influence of Economic Incentives on Work and Retirement* (1990). He received his Ph.D. in economics from the University of Chicago.

Gerben DeJong is Director of the National Rehabilitation Hospital Research Center in Washington, DC, and Professor in the Department of Family Medicine at Georgetown University's School of Medicine. He has written extensively on health, disability and income policy issues. He has experience in state income assistance programs and has conducted numerous studies on health and disability issues over the last 20 years. His works include: "Physical Disability and Public Policy" (in *Scientific American,* 1983); *Economics and Independent Living* (1985); and "America's Neglected Health Minority: Working Age Persons with Disabilities" (in *Milbank Quarterly,* 1989). In 1985, he received the Licht Award for Excellence in Scientific Writing from the American Congress of Rehabilitation Medicine. He received his Ph.D. in public policy studies from Brandeis University.

James N. Ellenberger is Assistant Director of the Department of Occupational Safety and Health for the AFL-CIO. He represents the federation on disability issues and workers' compensation. He co-chairs the Labor-Management Discussion Group on Workers' Compensation. He has written on a wide variety of subjects for various publications, including articles on disability policy, social insurance, health reform, and international labor and management issues. Mr. Ellenberger received his bachelor's degree from San Francisco State University and is a Certified Employee Benefit Specialist.

Lex Frieden is Senior Vice President of the Institute for Rehabilitation and Research and Professor of Physical Medicine and Rehabilitation at Baylor College of Medicine in Houston. He also currently serves as Vice President for North America for Rehabilitation International. From 1989-1993, he served as Chair of the Advisory Board for the National Center for Medical Rehabilitation Research at the National Institutes of Health. As Executive Director of the National Council on Disability from 1984-1988, Mr. Frieden was instrumental in developing the analyses and advocacy leading to the Americans with Disabilities Act of 1990. Working in the independent living movement for people with severe disabilities since the early 1970s, Mr. Frieden has published several books and papers on independent living. He has received two Presidential Citations for his work in the field of disability. Mr. Frieden received his M.A. in social psychology from the University of Houston.

Howard H. Goldman, M.D. is a Professor of Psychiatry at the Institute of Psychiatry and Human Behavior at the University of Maryland School of Medicine. He has extensive research publications on issues in public health, mental illness, and disability policy. He served on the American Psychiatric Association Work Group on the Diagnostic and Statistical Manual (DSM) IV (1988-93), the President's Task Force on Health Care Reform (1993), and the Social Security Administration's expert panel to update the mental impairment listings (1985). Among his many publications are: *Long-term Care for the Chronically Mentally Ill* (1983); "Cycles of Institutional Reform" in *Mental Illness and Social Policy* (1984); and *Inching Forward: A Report on Progress Made in Federal Mental Health Policy in the 1980's* (1992). He received his M.D. from Harvard University and his Ph.D. in social welfare research from Brandeis University.

Arthur E. Hess is a consultant in public administration, health care, and social policy. He has led a distinguished career in public service in the Social Security Administration, were he served as the Acting Commissioner of Social Security (1973-74) and the Deputy Commissioner of Social Security beginning in 1967. Mr. Hess was also the first Director of Health Insurance (Medicare, 1965-1967). As the first Director of Disability Insurance (1954-65), he developed the administrative structure for linking federal Social Security offices with state agencies for making disability determinations. He has consulted widely and received numerous citations for distinguished service, including a President's Award for Distinguished Federal Civilian Service. Mr. Hess received his A.B. from Princeton University and his LL.B. from the University of Maryland.

Thomas C. Joe is a social policy analyst focusing on the organization and delivery of human services, social insurance programs and income maintenance. He is the founder and Director of the Center for the Study of Social Policy. Mr. Joe served on the first National Council for the Handicapped in 1982, was instrumental in developing the nation's SSI program and helped two administrations draft welfare reform plans for families in poverty. He served as Special Assistant to the Undersecretary of the Department of Health, Education and Welfare, and subsequently served as consultant to the White House Domestic Policy Council. Mr. Joe received his M.A. in political science from the University of California, Berkeley.

Mitchell P. LaPlante is Associate Adjunct Professor in the Department of Social and Behavioral Sciences, and the Institute for Health and Aging at the University of California, San Francisco. He is also Director of the National Disability Statistics Rehabilitation Research and Training Center. He has written extensively on conceptual and definitional issues in disability, the demography and epidemiology of disability, and disability policy. Among his publications are: *Data on Disability from the National Health Interview Survey, 1983-85* (1988); contributor in *Disability in America: Toward A National Agenda for Prevention* (1991); "The Demographics of Disability" (in *Milbank Quarterly,* 1991); and *Disability in the United States: Prevalence and Causes, 1992* (1996). Professor LaPlante received his Ph.D. in sociology from Stanford University.

Douglas A. Martin is Special Assistant to the Chancellor at the University of California, Los Angeles, and as one of the original national pioneers of the independent living movement, co-founded the Westside Center for Independent Living in Los Angeles. His extensive knowledge of the Americans with Disabilities Act and the work incentive provisions of the Social Security disability insurance and Supplemental Security Income programs distinguish him as a leading scholar in disability studies. He is a founding member of the Society for Disability Studies and helped develop the research agenda for the National Institute on Disability and Rehabilitation Research, under the U.S. Department of Education. He was instrumental in the creation of a host of Social Security work incentive amendments including the SSI Section 1619 legislation. Mr. Martin received Ph.D. in urban studies from the University of California, Los Angeles.

David Mechanic is Director of the Institute for Health, Health Care Policy, and Aging Research and the René Dubos Professor of Behavioral Sciences at Rutgers University. He is also the Director of the NIMH Center for the Organization and Financing of Care for the Seriously Mentally Ill. As a recognized expert in mental health issues, he served as Coordinator of the Panel on Problems, Scope and Boundaries for the President's Commission on Mental Health and as vice chair of the Institute of Medicine's Committee for Pain, Disability, and Chronic Illness Behavior. Among the books he has written are: *Future Issues in Health Care: Social Policy and the Rationing of Medical Services* (1979); *From Advocacy to Allocation: The Evolving American Health Care System* (1986); *Mental Health and Social Policy* (3rd Edition, 1989); and *Inescapable Decisions: The Imperatives of Health Reform* (1994). Professor Mechanic received his Ph.D. in sociology from Stanford University.

Patricia M. Owens is President of Integrated Disability Management at UNUM America. She is responsible for developing new linkages of disability, health and workers' compensation programs and for overseeing research on disability issues at UNUM, and she coordinates an ongoing study of the full employer-related costs of disability to identify better risk sharing and risk management solutions. She has consulted with numerous employers assisting in compliance with the Americans with Disabilities Act and improved management of psychiatric disabilities. She served as Associate Commissioner for Disability of the Social Security Administration (1982-86), and was awarded the Health and Human Services Distinguished Leadership Award and a Social Security Commissioner's Public Service Citation for management of the disability program. Ms. Owens received her M.P.A. from the University of Missouri.

James M. Perrin, M.D. is Associate Professor of Pediatrics at Harvard Medical School, and Director of Ambulatory Care Programs and General Pediatrics, Pediatric Service, at the Massachusetts General Hospital. He serves as chair of the Committee on Children with Disabilities of the American Academy of Pediatrics and served on the expert panel for the Social Security Administration to establish eligibility criteria for the SSI childhood disability program to comply with the Supreme Court decision in *Sullivan v. Zebley.* He also served on the congressionally mandated National Commission on Childhood Disability (1995). A recognized expert in the field of pediatrics and chronic conditions, Dr. Perrin has published widely on the issues of chronic illnesses and public policies affecting children and disability. Some of his works include: "Reinterpreting Disability: Changes in SSI for Children" (in *Pediatrics,* 1991); *Home and Community Care for Chronically Ill Children* (1993); and "Health Care Reform and the Special Needs of Children" (in *Pediatrics,* 1994). He received his M.D. from Case Western Reserve University.

Donald L. Shumway is co-director of "Self-Determination for Persons with Developmental Disabilities," the Robert Wood Johnson Foundation Project at the Institute on Disability at the University of New Hampshire. A leading advocate for people with developmental disabilities and those with mental illness, Mr. Shumway is managing a nationwide grant-giving and technical assistance program involving health care and long-term care needs in a managed care environment. Formerly, he was Director of the Division of Mental Health and Developmental Services in New Hampshire, and was appointed by the governor to assume overall responsibility for the division's statewide system of institutions and community services for persons who have mental illnesses, developmental disabilities, or are homeless. New Hampshire became the first state to completely close its institutional levels of care and develop an integrated system of community supports. Mr. Shumway received his M.S.S. from Bryn Mawr College.

Susan S. Suter is the President of the World Institute on Disability. Ms. Suter has held several leading positions in the rehabilitation field including Commissioner of the Rehabilitation Services Administration, U.S. Department of Education (1988); Director of the Illinois Department of Rehabilitation Services (1984-88); Director of the Illinois Department of Public Aid (1988-89); and Director of the Illinois Department of Children and Family Services (1991-92). A distinguished and active expert in the disability community, she consults widely on issues involving the Americans with Disabilities Act, human resources and other employment issues. Ms. Suter received her M.A. in clinical psychology from Eastern Illinois University.

Eileen P. Sweeney is Director of Government Affairs at the Children's Defense Fund. Previously, she was a staff attorney with the National Senior Citizens Law Center, where she specialized in Social Security and SSI, and at the Legal Assistance Foundation of Chicago. She is a recognized expert in the field of administrative law, particularly the Social Security programs where she served as co-counsel on several cases. She is an effective advocate for children, the elderly, people with disabilities, and those in poverty. She also served as a member of the SSI Modernization Panel (1992), which was charged to examine the fundamental structure and purpose of the SSI program. Ms. Sweeney received her J.D. from Northwestern University.

Jerry Thomas is the President of the National Council of Disability Determination Directors. He is also the Director of Adjudicative Services for the state of Georgia. He has spent over 20 years in the state disability adjudication agency in various positions. He is a member of the Social Security Administration's Disability Redesign Advisory Council, a member of SSA's National Disability Issues Group, and has represented state disability agencies on many national panels and work-groups. He received his M.S. in political science from Florida State University. Mr. Thomas replaced Charles Jones on the Panel in July of 1994.

Abbreviations

ADHD	attention deficit hyperactivity disorder
AFDC	Aid to Families with Dependent Children
C-GAS	Global Assessment Scale for Children
CAFAS	Child and Adolescent Functional Assessment Scale
CDR	continuing disability review
CFR	Code of Federal Regulations
CSHCN	Children with Special Health Care Needs
DDS	disability determination service
DICA	Diagnostic Interview of Children and Adolescents
DISC	Diagnostic Interview Schedule for Children
DSM	Diagnostic and Statistical Manual
EPSDT	Early and Periodic Screening, Diagnosis and Treatment
GED	general equivalency diploma
GAO	U.S. General Accounting Office
IDEA	Individuals with Disabilities Education Act
IEP	individual education plan
IFA	individualized functional assessment
IFSP	individual family service plan
K-SADS	Kids' Schizophrenia and Depression Schedule
RFC	residual functional capacity
SGA	substantial gainful activity
SSA	Social Security Administration
SSI	Supplemental Security Income
U.S.C.	United States Code